TELLURIDE

TELLURIDE:
From Pick to Powder

by

Richard L. and Suzanne C. Fetter

The CAXTON PRINTERS, Ltd.
Caldwell, Idaho 83605
1990

First printing June, 1979
Second printing September, 1982
Third printing September, 1990

© 1979 by
The Caxton Printers, Ltd.
Caldwell, Idaho

Library of Congress Cataloging in Publication Data

Fetter, Richard L   1943-
    Telluride : from pick to powder.

    1. Telluride, Colo.—History. 2. Telluride,
Colo.—Description—Tours. I. Fetter, Suzanne,
1945-   joint author. II. Title.
F784.T44F47   978.8'23   77-87369
ISBN 0-87004-265-3

Printed and bound in the United States of America by
The CAXTON PRINTERS, Ltd.
Caldwell, Idaho 83605
152361

This book is dedicated to the people of
Telluride, past and present.

Contents

Page

FOREWORD 9

PART I: TO HELL YOU RIDE! 11

PART II: THE TOWN WITHOUT A BELLYACHE . . . 99

PART III: "SOMETHING BEAUTIFUL AND
CONSTRUCTIVE" 159

PART IV: A WALKING TOUR OF TELLURIDE 175

POSTSCRIPT 195

Foreword

One of the pleasures in writing is to tell a story. With history such pleasure is never total, for the tale remains incomplete the moment one stops writing.

In addition, there is always someone's relative or friend living in Las Vegas or elsewhere who knew another part of the story back in the early days. Nevertheless, the pieces must be put together the best one can. In this instance there were several people directly responsible for making the pieces available.

One such person is Arlene Reid, curator of the San Miguel County Museum in Telluride, who opened the museum to us and shared many stories of the town's past. Mrs. Reid also gave us access to her late husband's fine collection of old photographs, including many superb shots that he took himself. This book is undeniably richer because of her generosity.

For verification of uncertain facts and dates we consulted Don O'Rourke, Telluride's unquestionable authority, whose life in the town spans most of this century and whose tales could fill another book. Then there were people like Sandra Johnson and Alta Cassieto, Irene Wichmann, Spencer Trent of Greeley, Colorado; Evelyn Wagner, Elvira Wunderlich, and various individuals of the Telluride Corporation, all of whom gave time in one way or another to this project.

There were unknown people who stopped us on the

street to say, "Be sure to meet so-and-so. He can help you!" To all these people we express our sincere gratitude.

We received invaluable professional assistance from the staffs of the Denver Public Library Western History Section, the University of Colorado Western History Section, and the Colorado Historical Society.

Special appreciation also goes to John and Cathy Wrenn and Fran and Bill Coburn of Boulder, whose constant generosity and hospitality during those early summers of research facilitated our days in Colorado.

R.L.F.
Boulder, Colorado
November 1, 1977

I. TO HELL YOU RIDE!

It was an interesting rumor. John Fallon couldn't recall who had brought it to Baker Park (later to be known as Silverton), but word had drifted across the mountains that good placer claims had been found in the Marshall area at the headwaters of the San Miguel River. Fallon wasn't very interested in placer claims. These only let you mine the surface down to solid rock. It was grass roots mining — easy, valuable, but not a lode. A lode claim in those days gave the right to everything as far down as a man could dig. Your claim ran from the heavens above to the center of the earth, but where there were placers there might also be lodes.

Men were making great discoveries in Baker Park, but it looked as though Fallon wasn't destined to be one of them. He discussed the matter with his friend White, and the two agreed that it was time to move on. There was no way for them to know, but the rumor that caused their departure would make millionaires of unknown men during the two following decades and indirectly lead to the bombing of two Japanese cities to end World War II seventy-one years later.

The easier route from Baker Park to the Marshall Basin area in early 1874 was to head south to the Dallas Divide, then cross the divide and turn back east up the San Miguel Valley. Years before, however, the United States had signed a treaty recognizing the valley and the divide as territory belonging solely to the Ute Indians "for as long as the grass shall grow and the streams shall run." Under pressure from the government, the Utes had sold a large section of the mountains and ceded the mineral rights in 1873, but the foothills were still in their possession, as well as the mouth of the valley. The land was sacred to them, and no one crossed it without risking his life. Thus the easier route was across the Dallas Divide, but the only prudent route lay to the east of what is now Telluride — through the gorges, slabs of awesome rock, and the usually snowbound basins that form the amphitheater of mountains around the head of the valley. It was a treacherous passage, but the stories of Pike's Peak were then only fifteen years old, and men knew what great wealth might be found by those willing to endure a little hardship.

Fallon and White weren't the first prospectors to try the Marshall Basin area, nor were they the first to hear such rumors. As early as 1765 a party under the leadership of Juan Rivera had explored the area of the San Miguel River in search of silver and gold. Over the next eleven years other Spanish explorers came and left names for the region's mountains and rivers: the San Juan mountains for St. John; the Rio de San Perez, later named the Rio de San Miguel for St. Michael.

At the same time that a Declaration of Independence was being signed by the colonies back east, two friars named Escalante and Dominguez left Santa Fe with twelve men, probed the valley of the San Miguel as far as what would later become the location of Placerville, then crossed the Dallas Divide to the Uncompahgre and Gunnison rivers.

The route they followed became known as The Old Spanish Trail. This trail was later followed by the early American trappers and traders who first came out of St. Louis in 1831 to look for beaver. Their search took them well into the high country of the region, but the early explorers left no settlements behind when they departed. When the fur trade died out around 1840, the San Juans became a forgotten region until a detachment from Charles Baker's group went into the area in 1860–61. The detachment followed the San Miguel River up the valley to a point known as Howard's Fork, crossed the mountains over what came to be known as Ophir Pass, and returned to Baker's Park.

It was the treaty of 1873 and the ceding of mineral rights by the Utes that led to the early findings and subsequent rumors that brought men like John Fallon across the mountains. By 1874 men were coming from various parts of the Colorado Territory into the Marshall Basin and the high San Juans. These men, like Fallon, were looking for lodes. By the end of the year the sound of a pick in the basin area hillside was as common as the shrill cry of the marmots, and more than one skinny cottontail rabbit wound up in a hungry prospector's pan.

The winter of 1874–75 passed. It wasn't a particularly severe period, but no Colorado winter at nine thousand feet is ever pleasant. Fallon and the others emerged hardened by the cold and the storms but without a claim to record. Their search carried on well into the spring and summer before the mountains finally yielded to the constant picking, digging, and examining. Then, on August 23, 1875, the Remine brothers and a group of eight other men located and recorded the first placer claim in the San Miguel Mining District. The two brothers and their associates located a large part of the valley floor west of what would become Telluride, and the Remines settled down to live the rest of their lives in the valley.

Six weeks later John Fallon's long journey and his struggle through the cold winter were finally rewarded. On October 7 the clerk in the mining office took down volume one of the claim book, and on the bottom of page one John Fallon recorded the region's first lode claim. He called the claims the Emerald, Ausboro, Ajax, and Sheridan, or, as they came to be known, the

Sheridan Group. The importance of the discovery would be difficult to overestimate.

On Fallon's Sheridan Group would eventually be located the Mendota, the Smuggler, and the Union — claims which would produce millions of dollars worth of ore before the end of the century. The great vein of the Smuggler assayed at $1,200 per ton and, when combined with the Union, produced $18 million worth of ore by 1899, when an Eastern syndicate paid $15 million to obtain 51 percent of the property. At a time when freight rates on the nearest railroad were $60 a ton and miners' wages were $3 a day, ore from the Smuggler-Union gave its owners an immense profit.

Fallon worked his mine for a while, leased it in 1878 for two years, then sold it for $50,000 to a group from Milwaukee in 1880. His partner, White, didn't fare quite as well. Just as in Pike's Peak, Cripple Creek, and every other mining camp the world has ever known, Fortune would turn a cold shoulder on one man while smiling at another.

When Fallon staked out his claim and recorded it in October 1875, White went along to stake out extensions on the claims in hopes that his interest might turn up something worthwhile. For reasons unknown — fatigue, discouragement, a more exciting prospect — White neglected to do the minimum $100 assessment work as required by law, and he lost his legal rights to the claim.

In the meantime a man named J. B. Ingram had been poking around the Marshall Basin and had begun to suspect that the Sheridan and Union claims might be exceeding their legal allowance of 1,500 lineal feet. Ingram made a careful measurement of the claim and found that he had been most certainly correct. He then placed his own stakes on the illegal excess, strode down to the title office, and, with the glee of a pirate, filed a claim on the best-named mine in the basin, the

The Sheridan, part of the first recorded lode claim in the Telluride Area. Out of the awesome harshness of the Sheridan's surroundings would come millions of dollars in ore by the turn of the century.

Smuggler. For lack of a little assessment work, White lost a fortune.

The mining ledger filled rapidly with men's recorded hopes. Shortly after John Fallon located the Sheridan Group, Charles Savage, for whom an entire basin would be named, located the Argentine Group. On September 12, 1876, James Carpenter and Thomas Lowthian located the Pandora a mere two miles out of town. The Alta was claimed by Allen, Knot, and Dimick on July 25, 1877. By 1880 the Black Bear, Cimarron, Silver Bell, Liberty Bell, "46," and many other claims had been filed in the title office. A mining map of the period portrays a complex tangle of claims that

overlap and shoot off in all directions. Interests
changed hands or lapsed every day. It was a situation
that would have tested the skills of the finest lawyers,
had any been around. With each transaction and tap of
a pick, someone's hopes went sky high or fell to pieces.

Of all the mines, it was Ingram's Smuggler on
Fallon's Sheridan and Union claim that brought men
running. Its first shipment, brought out on donkeys for
rail movement east, was said to have brought $10,000.
Out across the plains and on to the East Coast word
passed quickly that things were happening again in the
goldfields of Colorado. Ingram's Smuggler Mine and its
$1,200-a-ton vein became widely known long before

Courtesy of the Homer Reid Collection

The Pandora, located in 1876 by Carpenter and Lowthian a mere two miles out of town.

Photograph by Richard L. Fetter

The boardinghouse at the Alta, today, a century after the mine was founded, is one of the area's most popular ghost towns.

the names San Miguel, San Juans, and Telluride acquired significance in the mining world. For years the early locator of a prospect used the word "Smuggler" to entice possible purchasers of his claim. The fact that the claim lay only a short distance in a certain direction from the Smuggler was a weighty argument to present to a potential buyer, and many lodes with very promising surface croppings were passed by in the search for a vein whose characteristics resembled those of the Smuggler.

In the entire exploding basin and valley there was but one problem, and that was transportation. By 1880 many of the mines had been located, but they weren't being worked extensively. The area had no tramways or mills. Mines that did work had as many sorters as miners. To meet all expenses, ore that was shipped had to be worth $300–$400 per ton. It was packed over the range to Ouray on burros, then by ox teams to Alamosa, and from there by rail to Grant Smelter in Denver. Power for mining was also a serious problem. Hoists and water pumps had to be operated in some of the mines with steam produced by burning wood, which was becoming scarce in some places. In short, the wealth was there, but it was a long, hard way to the bank.

We gain some insight into just how isolated the area was in 1880, and how hard to get in or out, in the experiences of W. J. Webb of Wisconsin. Webb left Wisconsin with a group of men from Trempeauleau County that spring. After many days of traveling across the

Courtesy of the Denver Public Library Western History Collection

The fabulous Smuggler, later to be joined with the Union, was loftily perched and ever more loftily valued. Its $1,200-per-ton vein was known from coast to coast, and its name was better known at first than Telluride, San Juans, or San Miguel. It produced $18 million worth of ore by 1899, when an Eastern Syndicate bought the controlling interest for $15 million.

Courtesy of Homer Reid Collection

The Smuggler mill and cyanide plant at a later date

Reliance on animals was great in the early days. The burro, mule, horse, and ox were the means of transportation of men and ore. This mule train is loaded with powder for one of the mines.

plains and the new state of Colorado, they arrived in Silverton and inquired about the condition of the trail over the mountains to Ophir, a distance of fourteen miles. There was a second, less direct route that climbed over the Dallas Divide and up the San Miguel Valley. The Utes had given up the valley completely by then, and no dangers remained except natural ones. It was three times as far over the divide, and many men, like Webb, opted for the shorter and less convenient route directly over the mountains.

They learned from the mail carrier that they could get through without snowshoes if they started early in the morning. Since neither Webb nor the man who was going over the pass with him knew much about snowshoes, they decided they could get along without them. A departure time of four in the morning was agreed upon, and the pair packed a light lunch, since the land-

Horse-drawn wagons hauling ore from the Tomboy Mine. Ore had to be worth $300–$400 per ton to justify selling to Grant Smelter in Denver. Transportation and power services were two of the great problems to arise by the early '80s.

lord wasn't about to get up before eight to prepare breakfast.

All went well for the first three or four miles, but the snow became deeper as they gained altitude and softer as the sunlight warmed the day. Soon the men were compelled to creep on their hands and knees and push their bundles ahead of them. In this way they reached the top of the pass, a distance of ten miles, at nine o'clock in the evening. They were 1,500 feet above timberline, without food, and "as near played out as the general run of men would have been at that stage of the game."

In order to keep from freezing they dug a hole in

the snow and crawled inside. The snow was four or five feet deep, and the men managed to spend the night comfortably enough to feel rested in the morning but "rather gaunt." They rolled up their blankets and started down the mountain on their knees for Ophir, four miles below. At 11:30 they arrived in town and promptly ordered something to eat, not having had much food during the preceding thirty-two hours. After spending the night in Ophir they set out for Telluride the following morning when, "finding the trail good and there but little snow," they "reached the flourishing town of Telluride in good seasons."

What Webb referred to as Telluride in his reminiscences years later was then a small town known as Columbia. The change of name occurred in 1881 at the request of the postal authorities, to help them solve the confusion of two Columbias. The other was also a mining camp, and even though it was in California there seemed to be a problem.

According to an edition of the *Mining Industry* in 1888, the name Telluride was chosen because a prospector on the San Miguel River found a great chunk of quartz which was more than half metallic gold. In his excitement he declared he had found telluride, an ore usually bearing rich mineral deposits, then thought to be the richest and most desired of all ores. At the place where the prospector made his find, according to the authority in 1888, the town of Telluride was established.

Whether or not the story is true, evidence does indicate that the town took its name from the highly sought ore. A more tenuous version is that the name is a contraction of "To Hell You Ride!" which was what a man was often told when he was setting out for the remote area. In spirit, if not fact, there is little to contest.

The Columbia that Will Webb found was one of two towns in the valley. Shortly after the first strikes were

made, a camp called San Miguel was begun a few
miles from the site of Columbia. The town grew
quickly. Before long a post office, a prestigious addition to a camp, was established, and several bars were
set up. San Miguel formally became founded as a town
on October 10, 1877. Shortly after, due to men pouring
into the valley, the camp called Columbia arose. A
rivalry developed between the two places, each trying
to attract newcomers. Frank Brown, who along with the
Remine brothers had been in the valley since 1873,
was one of the early pioneers who had hopes that San
Miguel would become the leading town of the valley.

Columbia had certain advantages. Most significantly, it was a few miles closer to the mines. There

Courtesy of Denver Public Library Western History Collection

"There was something about those wide streets where a team of six or eight oxen
could turn around without difficulty." Telluride's openness was one of the factors
that led to its being favored over San Miguel as the valley's leading mining town.

was also something attractive about its wide streets, where a team of six or eight oxen could turn around without difficulty. Every day there was a bustle of activity in town, and it seemed that the air was electric with high hopes. Burro trains were packing ore over the mountains to Ouray every day, and everyone seemed to feel Columbia was the only place to be. On January 10, 1878, the town was officially located and plotted as consisting of some eighty acres in a park six miles long and half a mile wide in San Miguel Valley.

The *Ouray Times* of June 12, 1880, was quite in agreement with Will Webb's conclusion that the town was flourishing. After reporting that the elections for the town officers of mayor, clerk, and recorder, and trustees had just been held, the *Times* went on to note, "The town is soon to have a new store. Quite a number of lots have recently been located. Streets are being

Courtesy of San Miguel County Museum

"Civilizing influences," women and children, were in Telluride by 1880. This photograph carries the identification, "First Family to Telluride."

An official map of Telluride in 1888, ten years after the town was located and platted, reveals street names and a plan unchanged a century later. In 1881 a residential lot could be bought for a dollar, with change for two beers.

cleaned up in good shape, and the town is generally putting on airs." Three months later another civilizing event occurred when Mabel Redick became the first baby born there.

Webb wrote back to Wisconsin at one point to say that no fewer than twenty-six buildings had gone up in two months' time, and that more would have been built had there been enough lumber. Another visitor to the town in 1881 reported to the *Times* that the town "had greatly improved since our last visit. A year of prosperity has brought about a very striking appearance. The beautiful park in which the town is located has been trimmed up, and dwelling and business houses mark the line of streets, making it all a beautiful little town."

Without doubt, it *was* a beautiful town. Game abounded in the forests. Wild flowers covered the valley in the spring and early summer, and the cool summer nights changed the leaves by mid-September to a brilliant rash of orange and yellow. The mountains towered mightily on three sides, and under any rock might lie the beginning of a man's fortune.

Under the 1867 Homestead Act land was free to anyone who wanted to claim and work it. When the last of the Utes left the valley in 1880, men came into the area from all over. By the end of the year there were more than eight hundred men in the valley and surrounding hillsides. Determined to become the leading town, Columbia offered irresistibly low prices to incoming settlers. A corner lot on main street in 1881 could be bought for $25, an inside lot for $5. If you were seeking a simple little residence lot, you could pay a dollar and receive enough change for two beers. The combination of natural beauty and local determination paid off. When the county of San Miguel was created on February 23, 1883, from the western part of Ouray County, Columbia was chosen to be the county seat.

Of course, not everyone found life in the town or camps to his liking. For men new at fortune-seeking there was a long period of adjustment. Will Webb recalled that during the first summer they had no potatoes, and he remembered with great distaste the condensed milk they bought at Brown's store in San Miguel as a substitute for cream. He ate so much venison during the first few years that he never cared for it again.

Most of the men who went west to seek gold did not find Fortune waiting at the mountain to bestow gifts as she had for Fallon and Ingram. For the majority, the only tales that drifted back across the plains were contained in letters home that often increased in despair as the hard months passed.

The *Trempeauleau County Messenger* of August 4, 1881, printed a note that was often repeated in many places throughout the country in the '80s: "James Brisco, who went out to Colorado last spring with 'the boys' from here, will return next November and take his old place in Camp's Store. Jim says there are places worse than Wisconsin to live in, and one of those is where he is staying in Colorado."

Will Webb, who was of Brisco's party, wrote from San Miguel to say there had been a snowstorm on July 3. He said there was no work, and board cost $1 per day. "The boys are becoming discouraged and getting homesick," he added, "one being credited with the remark that he wouldn't stay there for a year for all the gold in Colorado."

A man's fortune may have been lying under a rock, but Webb, for one, never found a place where a miner could just go and pick up gold nuggets. The veins had a way of pinching out after they were discovered. Even much of the grass-roots gold pinched out instead of gaining depth. Furthermore, the capital needed to get a mine started was far greater than most men had.

Shipments worth $10,000? Veins worth $1,200 per ton? That information got out quickly, but they didn't tell you that unless there was solid rock for a natural roof and sidewalls you had to cut white pine into planks and place the planks slanting along the walls to relieve the pressure. They didn't say much about the men hurt in cave-ins during the process. Or maybe they did but you weren't interested in that part.

There were lots of tricks to learn about mining. They used birds, rats, or mice to find out whether the air was safe. If the bird or animal died after being in the mine awhile, a ventilating system had to be built. Galvanized iron was brought into town in sheets which were made into pipes by rolling them around logs. Burros hauled the pipes up to the mines.

The ore drilled out of the mine was taken by burro down to a stamp mill to be pounded into powder. On the return trip the burros would bring in fresh supplies. In later years, when heavier machinery was brought in,

Courtesy of San Miguel County Museum

A "go-devil," one of the early contraptions for providing power for the mines "go-devils" were used. These were stone boats on iron wheels that moved along a roller. Power was supplied by mules who were hitched to either end. The zig-zag trails up to the mines were so steep that, prior to go-devil days, the animals would often cover five miles to reach a point one mile down the slope. Webb stood by

Courtesy of Homer Reid Collection

"Lucky" miners who had solid rock for walls and a roof. Even under such conditions it was necessary to test the air by sending in a bird, or rat, or mouse and seeing whether it survived. There was still no guarantee against a cave-in.

helplessly one day as his own pet burro floundered in deep snow, missed his footing, and disappeared down the mountain never to be seen again.

A man without a horse or burro in the early days walked where he had to go. With hay at $90 per ton, a horse was a bit of a luxury. Webb and many other men sometimes walked seventeen miles to Placerville. On one of these trips in September 1881 Webb heard from the stage driver just in from Gunnison that President Garfield had been shot. On another occasion he walked sixty miles to Montrose for supplies, but before too long the men were able to get most of what they needed in town.

It was a hard, often cold, usually inconvenient existence, far removed in both time and comfort from the rest of the country. Nevertheless, for every man who returned home to an easier life, there were twenty-five who couldn't tear themselves away from thoughts of what those awesome mountains most certainly hoarded in abundance. There was ample proof in the Marshall Basin of Pope's often-quoted observations, "Hope springs eternal in the human breast," just as there was for his lesser-known couplet:

The soul, uneasy and confined from home
Rests and expatiates in a life to come.

By 1881 there were enough people in the valley and enough happenings to prompt F. E. Curry to start the area's first newspaper. Curry's project began in San Miguel, but when he sold out to Charles F. ("Dad") Painter the following year, the newspaper was moved to Columbia. Charles Painter had come to Columbia in June 1880, and over the next sixty-three years he grew to be a well-liked, respected member of the town. Besides working as editor and publisher of the first newspaper, the *Journal*, he also served as the first mayor and first county clerk and recorder. Although he owned the

Office of the San Miguel *Examiner,* one of Telluride's early newspapers and print-ing offices. Telluride's first newspaper, the *Journal,* was begun by "Dad" Painter in June 1880.

Journal until 1927, most of his life was spent in the business of title abstracts and insurance. The old desk he used, as well as the big painted safe in which he kept deeds and documents for over half a century, are still in use on the main street (Colorado Avenue) at the San Miguel Title Company. More than thirty years after his death, employees still refer to him reverently as "Dad" Painter.

Painter put out the first edition of the *Journal* on March 11, 1882, after sweeping four inches of snow off the bed of the press. It hadn't been intended as an open-air press. The type and stands had been set up in a log cabin on the ground now occupied by the Sheri-dan Hotel. During the week while the building was being erected, type was set in the cabin. The original building was on the lot next to where the Silverjack now stands; the cement base of the old press is visible in the empty lot to the east. While the original building was going up, a snowstorm covered the bed of the press. This was swept off, and a box stove was set up and put in operation directly under the press. The message of the first issue was clear: "If you can't or don't want to work your mine, lease it to someone who does. If you can't get a percentage of the product, give it all to someone to work the mine, but have the mine worked at all event." The advice was sound enough to be reprinted by the *Journal* more than half a century later in 1935.

The year 1881 also marked the beginning of the first school. This too started in San Miguel in the home of Charles Jeff for a three-month summer term. In the fall,

Courtesy of Homer Reid Collection

"Dry Creek Cowboys at Dinner"

Superintendant Knapp requested that a school district be designated. When the request was granted, the area was known as Ouray County District No. 6. Miss Lillian Blair was hired to teach a three-month term during the winter of 1881–82, but the location for the school had been changed to Telluride. With an enrollment of thirty-seven, Miss Blair taught through the winter in a house owned by A. W. Taylor on the current site of St. Patrick's Church. On July 10, 1882, the district hired Miss Ella Billingsley to teach a term that was extended to five months, for which she accepted a salary of $55.

When San Miguel County was created in 1883, the school district designation was changed to San Miguel County School District No. 1. A school building was needed. An election was held, and a $3,000 bond issue was authorized. A one-room schoolhouse was built, with one teacher for fifty-three students. This served

Courtesy of Homer Reid Collection

The first school, 1881

the town's educational needs during the '80s. The building, now Telluride's City Hall, stands today on its original site.

A fire destroyed county school records in 1884, — not that there were very many to burn. Another fire razed the first courthouse shortly after it was built in 1885. The second courthouse, constructed with bricks from its predecessor, was built in 1887 on the main street, where it remains very much in use today. The courthouse of 1887 was an important, diversely used building. Dances, lectures, shows, meetings of all kinds, church affairs, and even services were held there.

It wasn't until two years later that a church was built in the valley, but religious services had been conducted from the time the town was founded. Two of the first men responsible for services in Columbia were the Reverend Mr. Ley and Parson Hoge. The Reverend Mr. Ley, born in 1845 in Tifflin, Ohio, was ordained in 1882 and assigned to Silverton in 1884. His responsibility included Animas Forks, Lake City, Ouray, Telluride, and Ophir, an area which today covers five counties.

The reverend's typical trip to Telluride from Silverton would be through snow, frequently at night. He would usually have to wrap himself in blankets and sleep in the snow to make the journey. He made many lonely trips in this manner to render aid to the sick and dying. On one trip he left Silverton on a Saturday night and didn't arrive in Telluride until Tuesday morning, due to the amount of snow on the pass. More than once he broke camp to find tracks where mountain lions had prowled while he slept.

Parson Hoge also came over from Silverton to hold meetings every Sunday in Jim Hurley's Corner Saloon on Pine Street and Colorado. Prior to construction of the courthouse, Hurley's upstairs room was used for of-

The courthouse, built in 1887, is a grand reminder of early days. Originally it served as a general meeting hall, for dances, and even church dinners, as well as for court matters.

fical courthouse affairs. Parson Hogg would enter the saloon and drape a sheet over the bar. All the gambling tables would close, and the men would listen respectfully to what he had come so far to say. After the meeting, Brounley Lee would help take up the collection. Lee, a gambler, talked through his nose in colorful and persuasive language. Though not particularly biblical, his techniques filled the hat each week. Following the meeting business would resume, and the parson would buy a stack of chips with the offering to see if he could double his collection before heading back to Silverton.

Prior to the establishment of any religious organization there were periodic visits by the Salvation Army. Braving the heights of the passes and the remoteness of the area, the determined band would appear on payday in front of the National Saloon. Four or five girls would dress up for the occasion and start singing to attract the miners. When the crowd got big enough they circulated and watched gold pieces of all shapes and sizes drop into their tambourines.

In 1889 the Congregational Church was organized in the town, "that style of denomination having been chosen because it allows its members the largest broadness of belief and makes nothing of dogma, creeds, or tradition; and also its system of absolute self-government fits the temperament of men and women who have progressive views and have no patience with the outside interference of conferences and synods."

One church? A free-wheeling, liberal, "progressive" town like this with only one church? Of course! "The fact that any given place has a multiplicity of churches does not necessitate that it is a specially religious community; very often it is quite the opposite, and conversely the statement that Telluride has only one church does not necessarily imply that we are, for that reason, irreligious, but it does show, and that to our credit, that we are not stupidly and doggedly denominational." No wonder that was the era of "rugged individualism"!

The one church that did exist was well in keeping with a town that was "putting on airs," and it was quite the pride of the town. It boasted of an audience room "fitted with massive seats of the latest pattern and carpeted in every part," a choir transept complete with organ valued at several hundred dollars, a lecture room, and a school beneath the church. The entire structure was eventually wired electrically and fitted with stained-glass windows. The people noted with some pride that its listed property value was $13,500.

Another aspect of civilization, a band, had long been part of the life of the town. By 1884 the *Journal* could report that the trip to Rico, with its pleasures and hardships, was a "very generally known" event. The pleasures included the good food and warm hospitality of the hosts at Rico, all of which compensated for the fact that band members made the trip on foot, horns strapped on their back, usually through enough snow to require wearing snowshoes.

Such things as schools, churches, county buildings, and musical groups had their place. They were needed; they made life more pleasant. But a town needed an economy to live, and that meant transportation. It meant roads and communication with the outside world. It meant power for the hoists and pumps, supplies for the men and animals. Without these, the valley could not survive for very long, no matter what promise lay uncovered in its mountains.

While Charles Jeff and F. E. Curry were becoming involved with a school and a newspaper in San Miguel, the narrow-gauge Denver and Rio Grande Railroad was busy laying track on the land evacuated by the Ute Indians. By 1882 they had arrived to within forty-five miles of Telluride. New excitement arose at the thought of ending the valley's isolation; miners calulated new railroad costs compared with packtrain time and expense over the mountains.

Unfortunately the railroad was not able to push any closer. In the same year however, 1882, a freighter named Dave Wood engineered a road through the forest from Montrose, across Horsefly to Leonard, and on to Telluride. Wood, who began hauling goods out of Pueblo and followed the railroad west, had learned the value of hauling freight quickly when he transported 500,000 pounds of goods one day and made $5,000. "Wood's Cut Off" was designed to avoid the problems due to floods which frequently prevented shipments from going to Telluride from Montrose. The project cost $30,000 but cut traveling time between Montrose and Telluride by three hours and eliminated a full day from shipping time.

Courtesy of San Miguel County Museum

A freight train led out of Telluride by Dave Wood

Courtesy of San Miguel County Museum

Dave Wood, freighter. "Wood's Cut Off" cost $30,000 but cut travelling time between Montrose and Telluride by three hours and elminated a full day from shipping time.

Supplies started flowing into Telluride more easily, and ore began to move out faster. A wagon road via Placerville was also completed in 1882, and four-horse Concord coaches began to arrive daily. Stagecoach service was fast and efficient. The fifty-mile route was interspersed with three stations where fresh horses waited. In three minutes the change would be made and the stage would be on its way. The coaches had two compartments called boots. In the front compartment, under the driver's seat, was an iron chest for express and first-class mail. The rear compartment was for luggage, trunks, and boxes. Frequently the coaches were filled to capacity, with eight people inside and six to eight more back to back on top. When they arrived the "locals" would rush out to meet the stage, give a hand to the arrivals, and catch up on all the news.

Prior to completion of Wood's cutoff, the greatest toll-road proprietor of all, Otto Mears, had built his most famous road — now part of the Million Dollar Highway — from Ouray to Red Mountain, and then on to Silverton, in 1883. A road from Dallas to Telluride was part of the entire "Mears System of Toll Roads" which eventually comprised about 450 miles of roads in southwestern Colorado.

Tolls on the road from Dallas were approximately as follows:

Each vehicle with one span of horses, mules or cattle . . . $1
Each additional pair of draft animals attached . . . 25¢
Each horse or mule with rider . . . 25¢
Horses, mules, cattle, or asses driven loose, per head . . . 10¢
Sheep, hogs, or goats . . . 5¢
Travel for attendance at funerals . . . Free

The trip to Telluride from Montrose could be accomplished in two days.

Improved lines of transportation brought more people, and Telluride hummed every day with increasing activity. Saddle horses clip-clopped along the street every hour of the day and night, shuttling miners to and from the mines. If the stage wasn't arriving, a packtrain was pulling out. A common sight on the main street every morning was a packtrain lining the street, animals loaded with everything from cookstoves to piled hay. About all that could be seen of some burros were two ears in front and a tail in back. Others were laden with rails for tracks in the mines, lumber, and heavy timber. Freight teams and ox trains with trail wagons of five yoke and ten oxen to each wagon stretched from one end of town to the other. The bull-whackers, as the drivers were called, could crack a long bullwhip and flick a fly twenty feet away.

There were characters like Dutch George, the walking waterworks man who carried two five-gallon oil cans suspended from a yoke around his neck and delivered water to the saloons and businesses on the main street at 10 cents a can. The sidewalks were made

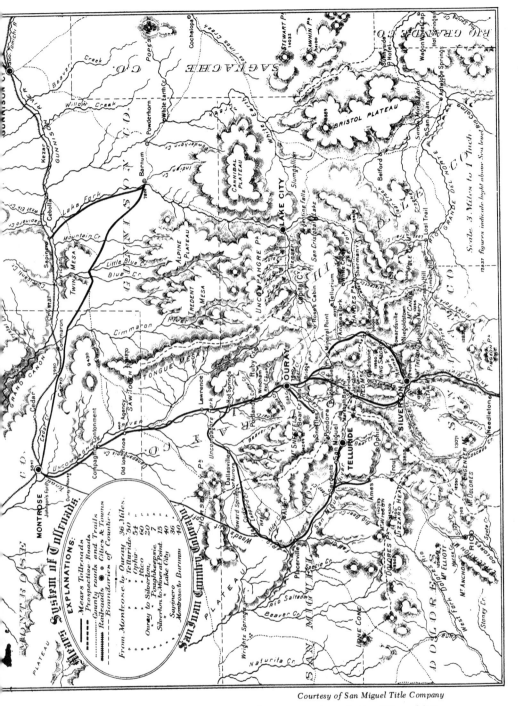

Courtesy of San Miguel Title Company

Otto Mears' Toll Road Network, constructed at various times in the '80s and '90s, amounted to 450 miles and laid the basis for today's "million dollar highway" out of Ouray, Colorado. The network included a road from Dallas to Telluride. Note Wood's cutoff out of Montrose.

of boards, bumpy with knots, and lined with hitching rails. Any miner desiring to go back to the mine, and in no condition to guide a horse, had only to get himself into the saddle, loop the reins over the saddle horn, and set the animal on its way. From the mine, the horse would wander back to the livery stable again.

Charles Painter's grandson, David Lavender, the prominent western historian, spent his childhood in Telluride and recalls one of the more unusual street scenes of the day. It concerned Dave Wood, the freighter, and his problem of taking a mile of unbroken cable to the Nellie Mine. Wood computed how many feet each mule could carry, then stretched the cable out in a long "U" down one side of the main street and up the other. Over the next two days he winched the cable into a series of coils four feet in diameter. Each coil weighed a certain amount, and there was one coil for

Courtesy of San Miguel County Museum

Colorado Avenue in the '80s, a time of activity and fervor — but not one relished by those with sensitive noses.

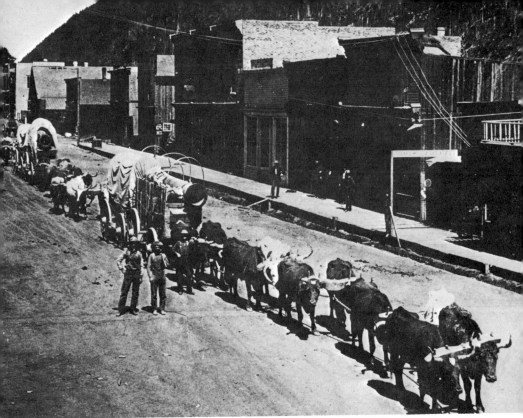

Telluride's main street; wagon trains, bullwhackers, and ox teams

Burros loaded with track iron for the mines

each mule with a length of slack in between. At dawn of the third day he led the mules between the lines of the "U," which even in coils covered more than a block. His packers lashed the coils to the saddles, and off they went, leaving two days of mule manure on the street for the city fathers and a lot a happily buzzing flies. Telluride in the early days was not a place a boy would forget.

The new lines of transportation if anything, served to increase the excitement of getting into the area. The Reverend J. J. Gibbons, successor to the Reverend Mr. Ley, crossed the Dallas Divide road many times and noted that for the most part the roads were good, "and even the most squeamish could make the trip without special risk of life or limb, save on the top of the pass. . . . Here for 300 yards you were compelled to take a trail that was always slippery from the constantly thawing snow. . . . Along the left of the trail was a steep precipice, and I noticed far down on a plain of rock several dead horses, but at the time I never thought of horses falling and rolling a quarter of a mile over the rocks. In going up the narrow trail my horse came to his knees several times, and, feeling unsafe, I dismounted and walked up the way leading to the pass."

The Reverend Mr. Gibbons wasn't the only one who chose to walk. Lots of miners found the $7 ticket on the stage from Dallas a bit too much to pay. Others walked, unashamed to admit they weren't trusting to anything but their own two feet to get over the top of the pass. As one miner described it, "One side was rocks, the other eternity." Among those who had the nerve and the money to take the stage, there must have been a lot of polite maneuvering to get the rock-side seats.

An important communication link was easily established in 1888 when a telegraph line was constructed which connected Telluride with Dallas and the line to

Courtesy of San Miguel
County Museum

"One side was rocks, the other eternity." Even where improved, the main road into Telluride was no place for squeamish stomachs or slippery feet.

Montrose and Ouray. Local businessmen required only a few hours to raise the money after C. E. Smith, night operator at the depot, told them the operation could be realized for $1,000.

While these changes were greatly altering the extremely isolated character of the valley, and certainly because of them, significant changes were also being made in ownership of the mines. The group of investors from Milwaukee who had purchased the Sheridan from John Fallon in 1880 decided to put the mine up for sale. J. H. Waters, a mining engineer employed by the Chinese government, had seen the Sheridan and had great confidence in the potential of the mine. When Waters heard it was for sale, he contacted a group of English and Scottish bankers and merchants living in Shanghai, and, over the course of the year, negotiated the purchase for the Shanghai syndicate. In 1883 the contract was signed, and once again the Sheridan changed hands. This time the price was $250,000, five times what the men from Milwaukee had paid Fallon in 1878.

The Shanghai investors retained Waters as general manager of the mine, and he resigned his post in China to move to Telluride. Waters proved to be an able man, who directed the operations of the mine with skill while adding significantly to his employers' holdings.

During the winter of 1887–88, he bought the Mendota mine, which lay north of the Sheridan. The owners, Donnellan and Everette, had staked it out in 1878 while holding the Sheridan lease from Fallon. The record of the Mendota, which operated modestly and conservatively, had been as good as that of the Smuggler and the Sheridan, and its purchase added considerably to the vast empire being constructed for the men in Shanghai. With the completion of the sale, Donnellan and Everette decided to take their profits and retire from mining in favor of influential real estate careers in Denver and Salt Lake.

Within months Waters closed an agreement for purchase of the Smuggler, and the Sheridan's famous neighbor to the south joined the list of syndicate holdings. Over the next few years the Pandora and Oriental lodes were acquired, as well as the Seventy-Six and the Bullion, all on the Smuggler vein, making six continuous and connecting locations on the one vein. On another vein which crossed the Smuggler diagonally, where the Union and Seventy-Six joined, the company had the Emerald and the Pennsylvania, plus numerous other lodes, locations, and placers.

Under the direction of Waters this vast network of mines was joined together with a famous cross-cut tunnel which was 3,470 feet long and intersected the main

Miners of the Sheridan. This picture, taken after the mine was sold for $250,000, probably portrays many of the men who built the famous 3,470-foot-long crosscut tunnel which intersected the main and adjoining veins 960 feet below the surface.

and adjoining veins at a depth of 960 feet below the surface. From the mouth of the tunnel an incline cable road connected with the mill and, eventually, the railroad below. The incline overcame a vertical drop of 2,460 feet and was itself 8,400 feet long. Its construction required the building of nine bridges, one with a span of 230 feet, and four tunnels, one of which was 470 feet long. It was this immense complex of tunnels, bridges, and rich veins that would be sold for $15 million within a decade.

Just before Waters began accumulating the holdings that would comprise the Sheridan empire, in 1886, another mine entered Telluride history. The Tomboy was claimed by Otis C. ("Tomboy") Thomas, who made the claim for George Rohwer. From the first, the Tomboy paid from the grass roots. It began as a gold

Photographs by Suzanne C. Fetter

Remains of the Tomboy today: weathered boards and scrap iron where once $2 million was paid to own the working railways.

mine, but later, when the Argentine was acquired, the operation was expanded to include the mining of silver and lead. After being combined with the Belmont, the Tomboy began to produce heavily in 1894, and it was sold for $100,000. Three years later it was reported sold to Rothschild's of London for $2 million.

According to legend, the Belmont had been bought originally for $5 by Mrs. Emily Costigan, who felt sorry for the owner because he was out of money. Whether true or not, the Tomboy could be depended upon to make money for its stockholders, which was not always true of the renowned Smuggler. The mine was associated with a number of significant people. One of these was Gelasio Caetanni, who examined the Montana Mine for the Tomboy Company prior to the Tomboy's purchase of the Montana. Caetanni was then with Burch and Caetanni, a firm of mining engineers in San Francisco. Caetanni returned to Italy during World War I and became the engineer who supervised driving the tunnels which played an important role in a battle between the Italians and the Austrians. Later he became Mussolini's first ambassador to the United States.

Some of the old-timers avowed in their later years that the Tomboy was one place where you had to clean up and wear some kind of jacket or coat in the dining hall. They also recalled how once a month the management would furnish a couple of stages to transport "strictly respectable" girls from Telluride for a dance. The "other kind" was around too, operating in a neutral strip between the Smuggler and Tomboy properties. Whatever else they did, the girls cost the two managements thousands of dollars spent trying unsuccessfully to run them out.

Maybe one side of the road into Telluride promised nothing but eternity, but at the end of the road there was beginning to be a lot of money. If a man were clever enough he might be able to obtain a fair chunk of it without getting his hands dirty. The town was becoming the place where dreams were made and, much later, Hollywood movies.

Early in the summer of 1889 three men arrived and set up camp on the mesa south of town. They kept their horses well fed and occasionally went to town to socialize with the miners. Over the course of a few weeks they learned a few things about the physical setup of the San Miguel Valley Bank and found out when payday would be coming around again.

On the designated day they rode into town, where they were by now familiar, looked around a bit, went to a saloon and bought a cigar each, and at twenty to ten rode past the bank and saw that the regulated time safe was open. The day before, $24,000 had been sent to Telluride for the miners' payroll.

Two of the men dismounted and strolled into the bank as if to make a transaction. The third waited outside, holding the reins of the other men's horses. The bookkeeper was just leaving for the post office with a package of letters, and only the cashier was left in the bank. The taller of the two men strolled up to his window and told him to put up his hands. The official turned around, looked, and started to laugh but changed his mind when a long revolver barrel was thrust under his nose. He threw his hands into the air. The second robber leaped over the railing and dumped the crisp new dollars into his gunnysack, along with all the gold he could find and a few silver dollars.

The cashier was threatened with death if he made a sound, and with that the two left the bank. During the whole robbery not a man happened to pass by or even be in sight. That they were cool in their daylight success may be judged by the remark, "Boys, the job is well done, and we have plenty of time. Keep cool now and let us be gone."

They rode up the street shooting their guns, perhaps as a warning to all those who might think about trying to capture them. The cashier finally got up enough nerve to peep outside and saw the bookkeeper returning from the post office. A ghostly white, he finally stammered out the news of the robbery.

Within fifteen minutes the chase was on, with a twelve-man posse in pursuit. Out near Wichmann's Brewery a cowboy who recognized the robbers joined the posse. His horse was swift, and soon he was too close to the bandits for their comfort. Tom McCarty, one of the robbers, got behind a huge rock, waited for the man, stepped out, and held him up. The cowboy was relieved of his pearl-handled revolver and admonished not to get so close again. All of this was to be denied later of course by Adsit, the swift pursuer who was embarrassed by his humiliating capture.

Later on, another member of the posse with a good horse got enthusiastic and shot out several hundred yards ahead of the others. Finding all of a sudden that he was a little too far from his buddies, he decided to answer a call of nature, which he did. He would not hear the end of that witty maneuver for years to come.

The race was close. This was evident a few months later when the carcasses of four horses were found still tied to a tree. They had been left for relay, but the outlaws had been crowded into a different getaway route and were unable to pick them up. The robbers did rest for a bit at Trout Lake but disappeared as soon as the posse got too close. They managed a change of horses between Rico and Dolores and kept the first string with them except for one fine brown horse which was unable to keep up. The sheriff took this horse and rode him for years.

Telluride and Rico were wild with excitement over

the robbery, but the Wild Bunch was never caught. One of the gang was later killed in a bank robbery at Delta, Colorado, and the others disappeared into Utah. The scene of the crime, the first of many for Butch Cassidy, still remains on the main street, an old white building standing next to the drugstore at the corner of First and Colorado Avenue.

A booming town like Telluride in the late '80s wasn't about to be put out of business by a little thing like a robbery, although the San Miguel Valley Bank had difficulty bouncing back. Between 1891 and 1900 the town had two banks, the First National Bank, now the BPOE Lodge, and the Bank of Telluride, which is the Greek-columned old building on the main street just up from Pine. Both banks had large capital and resources, with gold coin stacked two feet high on shelves. Interest was usually 1.5 percent a month, and no one bothered using pennies. If more than 2½ cents was in question a nickel would be used; amounts less than 2½ cents were forgotten. Miners, distrusting paper money, paid for everything in coin, and there are some who insist that the smallest coin in actual circulation was a quarter.

Times were excellent, but those who dared to look below the surface knew there was ample cause for concern. The old problem of fuel for the mines was becoming acute once again. The roads of Dave Wood and Otto Mears and the proximity of the railroad had enabled mines that had been nearly closed in the early '80s to continue operating successfully, but ten years had passed. Timber was now nearly exhausted, and coal delivered by burro was costing $40 to $50 a ton. In the early days it had been much easier. Timber was abundant, and there was a wealth of high-grade ore located near the surface. It simply had been a question then of hauling the ore sixty miles for milling. As time passed they had to dig deeper for low-grade ores, and it

Main street (Colorado Avenue) today. The small white building in the center of the picture, to the right of the drugstore, was the San Miguel Valley Bank. Where cars and jeeps now park, Butch Cassidy and the Wild Bunch lit out for Utah with $24,000 of Telluride's money.

became necessary to have mills on the spot. Power was the problem. If it hadn't been for the genius of L. L. Nunn and Otto Mears, Telluride might well have died before the turn of the century.

Early in 1890 the Gold King Mining Company near Alta Lakes was in the red and well aware of the reason. Times had changed. The company needed power for its mines. More out of desperation than confidence the owners went to L. L. Nunn, a five-foot one-inch firebrand who entertained wild notions of being another Napoleon. Nunn was practicing law in Telluride after having worked as a restaurateur in Leadville, where he also spent some time in the building business and made extra money by renting out his tin bathtub on Saturday nights. Nunn had distinguished himself on his arrival in Telluride by living in a tent, shingling roofs, existing on a diet of oatmeal, and walking from Telluride to Ouray and back in one day. Eventually he was able to start a law practice. Someone at the Gold King was able somehow to realize that, through all this, Nunn was also a genius.

It seemed to Nunn that some kind of electrical transmission was necessary, and he thought it would be possible to use the power generated by the South Fork of the San Miguel River. This fork came down from Ophir and fell more than five hundred feet in less than a mile. The amount of water could produce power for every mine around. Direct current could not be used, since the power was lost before it could reach its destination. Nunn had heard that alternating current could be carried long distances, and he gradually developed the idea of using alternating current transmitted at high voltage and then stepped down for use with transformers. Nunn's thoughts generated a lot of interest in town, but for most people they confirmed that the man really was an oddball.

Nunn had never been one to worry too much about public opinion. He went ahead and contacted his brother Paul, a good engineer, to look at the problem.

At the time, there was a dispute in the engineering and scientific world concerning the merits of alternating current, backed by George Westinghouse, as opposed to Thomas Edison's direct current. Even with Westinghouse's personal support, Nunn had a hard time persuading the Westinghouse board of directors to back the $15 million venture. Prompted by a telegram from Westinghouse saying that the board was on the verge of vetoing the project, Nunn left for Pittsburgh, went before the board, and laid out before the as-

L. L. Nunn, the eccentric genius who used alternating current for the generation of power. It was the first time this feat had been achieved anyplace in the world.

tonished men $100,000 in $10 gold pieces. "I'm willing to gamble that, gentlemen. What are you prepared to do?" Nunn asked.

The ploy had its desired effect, as did the announcement by the Gold King Mining Company that a vein worth $2 million in gold had been discovered. Although no one in the East or in Telluride paid too much attention, a contract with Westinghouse Electric and Manufacturing was signed, and Nunn returned to join brother Paul.

The two men and some associates went to work at once on the construction of the Ames Power Plant, which was equipped with a 3,800-volt generator. The problem now was to find workers who knew how to run his plant as well as to devise new equipment. There was only one school in the country with a good course in electrical engineering, and there was no such thing as graduate engineers looking for challenging work. Nunn also had to find men who were willing to ignore old theories and branch into areas totally new and untried. The problem was solved by the creation of the Telluride Institute.

Nunn took students from Cornell University in New York and young men interested in the West and set them down together to think. They climbed poles, strung wires, invented their own lighting arresters, took basic courses in machinery, and did shopwork in metal and wood, wiring, insulating, and repairing. The new students had a technical library and a testing room, and they called themselves "Pinheads." They learned as they went along, and Nunn paid them $30 a month plus room and board.

The Pinheads worked throughout the winter, sometimes in cold that reached 40 degrees below zero. They built a dam in the stream, laid 4,000 feet of iron pipe to conduct water from the headgate, and divided the stream toward two Pelton waterwheels. The brilliant electrical wizard, Nikola Tesla, designed the motor they used, and Westinghouse provided the generators. Writers of the day called the project "interesting," but most people who gathered for the opening the following spring were saying it couldn't be done. In a day when transportation was securely tied to the horse and mule, something moving at 186,000 miles per second was a little too much to accept.

Nunn threw a switch, and an arc jumped six feet into the air. Power surged through the line to the Gold King Mine three miles away. The 100-horsepower engine ran flawlessly, and those present witnessed the first example in the world of a power station transmitting alternating current at high voltage for power purposes. Two months later a similar experiment was successfully concluded in Germany. In Telluride, a place unknown to white men a mere twenty years before, a world's first had occurred.

The wildcat Nunn was now a pioneering genius. The big attraction on Sunday afternoon was to ride to Ames to watch the plant start up after the weekly shutdown on Saturday night. Miners would gather to watch what they couldn't believe was happening. They would ask how long it took the current to run uphill, give the generator a twist, and return. Even with it there before you, 186,000 miles per second was hard to believe.

Operating costs at the Gold King plunged from $2,500 to $500 a month, and by 1894 Telluride could make the extraordinary claim that the whole town as well as many of the mines and mills were electrically lighted. Low-grade ore that had been too poor to mine profitably now became worth seeking. The boost to the economy was immeasurable, and behind it all lay the genius of an oddball named L. L. Nunn.

Nunn's personal economic worth improved handsomely. But history was cruel to Nikola Tesla, the brilliant man whose patents were instrumental to the success of the venture and whose reputation is known to very few. The Pinheads survive in factual and tall tales in the finest Telluride style. One of the lighter (and truthful) moments occurred during the winter of 1891–92 when the students turned their attention to the problem of getting some snakes out of the powerhouse. The snakes enjoyed crawling in at night and couldn't be kept out because they had found a way through the wall where the operating shaft extended to the waterwheel. The electricians decided that if the snakes had to crawl over two metal plates they could be electrocuted. The theory was absolutely correct. Not only were the snakes eliminated, but the plant was closed due to short-circuiting caused by the experiment.

A more tenuous story is this: The Pinheads at Ames

received a call in September 1901 and were told to run
for their lives. Trout Lake Dam had broken, and a roar-
ing wall of water and timbers would soon be upon
them. Quickly the Pinheads dashed for a slide rule,
calculated the amount of water and the size of the canyon, and then hastened to the nearest telephone pole.
They climbed to the height they had figured was high
enough and waited. The water tore down the canyon,
surged to within three inches of their shoes, and sub-
sided.

The original power installation is now part of the
Western Colorado Power Company, a subsidiary of the
Utah Power and Light Company. L. L. Nunn's house
can be seen on the northwest corner of West Columbia
and North Aspen. Next to it stands a little house where
the students of the Telluride Institute lived, studied,
and solved the problems of alternating current and un-
wanted snakes.

Nunn provided the town and the mines with
needed power. Almost at the same time, Otto Mears
had undertaken to solve the problem of transportation.
In terms of sheer drama, courage, and significance to
Telluride and the surrounding area, nothing could
compare with Mears' building of the Rio Grande
Southern Railroad.

Otto Mears built his first road in 1867, a route over
Poncha Pass of about fifty miles which connected
Saguache with Nathrop in southern Colorado. At
Nathrop the road connected with the Denver-
California Gulch Road through South Fork. Maj. William Gilpin, appointed by President Lincoln in 1861 to
be the first territorial governor of Colorado, told Mears
that some day a railroad would be running over his
road. At the time there wasn't a railroad to Denver, and
Mears thought Mr. Gilpin was "a little crazy" to have
such thoughts. But the first governor of the territory

was far from being a fool. Mear's fifty-mile road became part of a 450-mile system of toll roads in the San Juans that is the basis of today's railroads and highways.

By 1889 Mears had connected much of southwestern Colorado with his roads. Included in his accomplishments was the spectacular road from Ouray to Silverton via Red Mountain, much of which was cut out of the solid rock of the Uncompahgre Canyon. On October 30 he formed the Rio Grande Southern Railroad with a group of prominent citizens that included the governor, and he set his sights on a project that would reach Telluride. The railroad was to be narrow-gauge, and the work would be done by the Rio Grande Southern Construction Company. To finance the venture, Mears sold a total of $9,020,000 worth of stocks and bonds in the company.

Telluride in fact would be but part of a great line that ran down through Rico, Dolores, and Mancos, to connect Ridgway with Durango. By June of 1890 Mears had 1,500 men blasting, shoveling, measuring, and constructing trestles out of Ridgway across the Dallas Divide. Using great portions of the toll road Mears had put in from Ridgway to Telluride across the divide in 1880, the crews were able to work rapidly toward Telluride. By October 10, trains were running twenty-seven miles to Placerville and by November 16, 38.5 miles to Vance Junction. By December 1 the section to Telluride, a distance of forty-five miles from Ridgway, was ready for use. At Telluride the tracks ran another 2.5 miles to the Pandora Mine.

From Vance Junction, where the branch line went in to service Telluride, the tracks ran south for six miles, hugging the cliffs that dominate the west side of the San Miguel Valley. At Ophir the valley ends abruptly, giving way to an escarpment which rises several thousand feet, blocking passage to the south. Mears' bridge gangs, powder crews, and construction men spent six months laying four miles of track which lifted trains, by way of the famous Ophir Loop, up to the rim of the canyon and on to Lizard Head. Four long trestles and a network of retaining walls and dangerous shelves cut out of solid granite held the tracks from Ophir Depot to Trout Lake. The section to Rico wasn't ready until September 31, 1891.

At the other end of the line, men had been laying tracks out of Durango at the rate of a mile and a half a day. The Rio Grande Southern was finally completed on December 17, 1891, when the final spike was driven at a spot eleven miles below Rico, 225 yards beyond milepost no. 77. The line had taken twenty-one months to build. One hundred thirty bridges had been constructed, the longest measuring 544 feet. The Ophir trestle was 95 feet high, and the entire "loop" measured 162.5 miles, not counting the small branches such as those to Telluride and the Pandora Mine. It is said that after his first trip over the hairpin turns and steep inclines of the Ophir-Telluride run, Mears returned by horse, saying, "I only build those things, I don't ride them."

At a time when banks didn't fool around with small change and miners were paid in hard coin, it was only fitting that a southwestern railroad tycoon from Colorado should celebrate the occasion appropriately. Colorado being "The Silver State," Mears made up a number of silver passes for his railroad, signed in the center with his name. The pass was rimmed with sterling silver, and inside the edge was frosted filigree on which in raised letters was written "The Rio Grande Southern R. R. — Pass — 1892. The donee's name was engraved in the center, along with the words, "Otto Mears, Pres't."

Mears also had a limited number of gold passes made. These were identical to the silver passes, except

The Rio Grande Southern crossing the Ophir Loop

they were made of one ounce of solid gold. Mears gave the silver passes to special friends. The four to six gold passes were for the big shippers. A few of both the silver and gold passes are in existence today as highly valued collector's items.

Otto Mears was in many respects as romantic as his railroad. He spoke fluent Spanish and Ute as well as English and was a great asset in bringing about treaties between the Utes and the whites, being respected by both as an honest man.

He came to America at the age of ten, having been born in Russia in 1840 and orphaned at the age of four. His mother's brother took care of him for a while then sent him to England, where another uncle sent him to

Courtesy of Homer Reid Collection

Workmen on the Ophir Loop — 95 feet high, connecting a passage through steep cliffs. The loop demanded six months of construction to lay four miles of track. At the Durango end of the line, men were laying a mile and a half of track per day.

A solitary boxcar awaits the train on the Ophir Loop

New York in the care of an old lady and the ship's captain. In New York another relation met him and took care of him for a time before sending him to one of four uncles in California. Again the boy was put in the care of a kindly old lady and the captain of a ship. When no uncle was in California to meet him, the lady took him to a boardinghouse. Mears sold newspapers, learned how to be a tinsmith, and eventually went to San Francisco where he slept in a room with twelve people and woke up to find his money gone.

Over the following years he drifted to the gold discoveries in Nevada, became a naturalized citizen, fought in the Civil War with the California Volunteers, and later fought the Navajos under Kit Carson. After he was discharged he set up a store and became involved with freighting and packing. Mears was growing wheat in Saguache, Colorado, when the government knocked down prices on wheat he had been supplying to Fort Garland. In order to find a better market, he used axes and shovels to build a road down to the Arkansas Valley, where he could obtain better prices.

It was at this point that William Gilpin came along and gave him the idea of tolling his road. Mears was off on a new career. For years he was the largest purchaser of hay, grain, and teaming animals in the Colorado Territory. He had thousands of drivers, teamsters, stable keepers, and carriers. He built a road to Lake City and installed a newspaper there. When Lake City boomed, people came in on Mears' roads that were there waiting for them. Nothing escaped his attention. When he decided Lake City had to have mail, he contracted with the goverment to take it in. In the middle of winter his couriers would take the mail in on a toboggan drawn by dogs, with one man alongside on Norwegian snowhoes. When Washington started receiving complaints about ladies' hats being crushed by men who sat on the toboggans, and when his carriers quit in March 1876 be-

A "doubleheader" similar to the one that took fifty dressed turkeys and three barrels of beer to celebrate at the completion of Mears' railroad in December 1891.

cause of deep soft snow, Mears took the mail in himself. After three days of hardship and sinking into snow at every step, he arrived with the mail as he had agreed. Then he had the trail opened, and the mail went regularly.

When the persevering Mr. Mears prepared to drive the final spike south of Rico in December 1891 it was a cause for tremendous celebration in Telluride and throughout the San Juans. In a special article from Durango, the Denver *Daily News* announced, "The last spike on the Rio Grande Southern will be driven tomorrow, and thus Rico, Telluride, and Ridgway will be united to the metropolis of the southwest. A doubleheader, drawing twenty cars of Durango coal from the Porter Mine, will leave Rico at 7 o'clock tomorrow morning. The train will be decorated appropriately and will make a through run. . . . The train that leaves here tomorrow will take fifty dressed turkeys and about three barrels of beer from the Durango brewery as a treat to the laborers on the track at the completion tomorrow."

The trains arrived by 2 P.M. After proper ceremonies were observed, a silver spike from the ore of David Schwichheimer's mine was driven into the ground. Inscribed on the spike were the words, "The Honorable Otto Mears, President" and "Silver from the Enterprise Mine." Upon completion of the ceremonies, liquor flowed freely, and the bands from Telluride and Rico outdid themselves.

In the evening a formal banquet and ball were held. The organizers had scoured the country for a chef with arts equal to the occasion. Mr. James Deti, who was present that evening, recalled years later, "Never before or since did the Enterprise Hotel cater to such a notable crowd or furnish such a sumptuous banquet. Otto Mears occupied the place of honor at the head of the table. Speech making was indulged in, each one being a little more elaborate than the one before but all promising great things for the community and the new railroad, the Rio Grande Southern.

"The ball began with the formal grand march, then came the lively quadrilles, Virginia reels, and polkas, also the graceful waltzes, 'souviennes, and schottisches. Here were the ladies in wasp-waisted, bustled gowns of the finest satins and silks and stately coiffeurs to match. Here were the males in stiff-collared, pleated shirts and clinging-legged trousers. Most of them had a facial adornment in the way of a microscopic waxed mustache or one of the handlebar type of more imposing proportions. This formal party came to an end at 3:30 in the morning."

Of course, Deti adds, "lesser citizens" were commemorating the affair with their own parties, and no saloon lacked for business or high spirits that night. The trains left the morning after the great affair at 5:15, 8:40, and 9:20 to take the weary celebrants home.

It was an occasion worth getting excited about. With the arrival of the railroad, business boomed in a way even the optimists hadn't foreseen. Before a month passed the railroad had to refuse to carry some merchandise simply because it lacked the capacity. Thirty-five locomotives puffed their way over Dallas Divide and Lizard Head pass with up to twenty freight loads a day. Passenger trains covered the entire road twice a day in each direction. By spring thirty miles of thirty-pound rail had been worn out between Vance Junction and Rico and was replaced with fifty-seven-pound iron.

All the glory, charm, and nostalgia involved with old-time railroading were embodied in those early years of the Southern. For years there were narrow-gauge sleepers with elaborately panelled interiors and silver-furbished Pintsch lamps, private cars of Telluride millionaires, and the elaborate cars for Mears himself and other road officials. Tourists from the East and visiting Englishmen in Dumdrearies and deer-stalkers interested in investing in Colorado properties became common sights on the Southern.

Congress passed the Sherman Silver Purchase Act in 1890, under which the government bought silver at $1.29 per ounce. When the act was repealed in 1893, the price of silver collapsed and mining was brought to a temporary standstill. The ensuing panic and recession hit the Southern hard, driving it into bankruptcy. Wages, which had always been good on the Southern, fell to below meager subsistence level. Employees once had to wait three months to get paid. The railroad went into receivership, with Mr. E. T. Jeffrey, president of the Denver and Rio Grande Southern, acting as receiver. On November 30, 1895, the Southern passed into the control of the D&RG, which eventually came to own about 70 percent of its stock. On December 1 the court terminated the receivership, and the Southern was free of indebtedness. It had changed, however, from being an independent railroad to a cog in the railroad empire of Jay Gould, which included the D&RG, the Missouri Pacific, the Texas and Pacific Wabash. The parent wanted to scrap it and habitually neglected it, but communities and industries along the route persuaded Congress to keep it open every time the crucial question of its existence was raised.

Going through the rugged terrain it did, and being neglected as well, the Southern was bound to have its share of dramatic accidents, which it had with alarming frequency and often with terrible consequences.

Despite the dangers and death the railroad chugged on. By the turn of the century tourists were crowding

Courtesy of Homer Reid Collection

The RGS in a quiet moment

Courtesy of San Miguel County Museum

"Frequently the Telluride Cornet Band would play for visitors" as shown in this 1886 photograph.

the cars of the Southern to gasp over shaky trestles and gawk at the splendor of the silvery San Juans. Frequently the Telluride Cornet Band would play for visiters, as evidenced by the painting in one of the soda-fountain booths at the present corner drugstore. Iceboxes were filled with beer and sandwiches, and locomotive smokeboxes would be draped with bunting for special outings. The pace was slow and casual, and the bumps and jolts were many. One of the many jokes in circulation concerned a lady expecting a baby who asked the conductor if the train could go just a little faster. "You shouldn't have gotten on in this condition," the conductor replied. "I wasn't in this condition when I got on," said the lady.

Another time the train from Rico to Dolores had only two passengers, a woman and a baby. The baby was crying because her milk had soured. Barney Gogarty, the conductor, pulled the cord, stopped the train, and went to a nearby farmhouse for some fresh milk. A few minutes early, a few minutes late, it didn't matter much on the Southern.

On one of the more businesslike occasions after the turn of the century, when prospective investors were being entertained in one of the luxurious cars of the Southern, Daniel C. Kackling proposed the mining of copper. Base metals weren't in vogue in those days and the *Engineering and Mining Journal* called his idea

Courtesy of Homer Reid Collection

Lizard Head, a famous landmark of the San Juans on the old railroad and now easily seen from Highway 145.

"wildcat." Some people in Cripple Creek supported him, however, and over the next forty-five years the Utah Copper Company mined six billion pounds of pure copper, making more and richer millionaires in consequence than Cripple Creek and Telluride combined.

One can only dream of the popular living reminder of the narrow-gauge era we would have today if the

". . . the line ran straight under the teeth of the San Juan Mountains for over fifty miles."

railroad were still running the "Loop." From Salida, where the tracks left the standard gauge, the line ran straight under the teeth of the San Juan Mountains for over fifty miles. At Durango there was the side trip to Silverton. From Durango, via the Mears Road, the tracks ran to the Rico mines, stopped briefly at Lizard Head to see the famous rock formation, then moved on to Trout Lake, the high trestles of Ophir, and Telluride. At Ridgway the Southern ended and connected with the Denver and Rio Grande. Travelers could continue over the road's first transcontinental narrow gauge through the Black Canyon of the Gunnison, over the Marshall Pass and back to Salida and standard gauge. Until about 1914, when the automobile began to affect the touring plans of a significant portion of the public, the great loop was as popular as any attraction in the West, including Yellowstone and the Grand Canyon.

Little remains of the Southern today. Pause along the way from Telluride to Rico and you will find track bed, or drive through the Uncompahgre National Forest by way of the Ilium road to Ames outside Telluride and you will find two old railroad cars standing wheelless in the weeds along the old roadbed. Nearby stands a former loading chute. Nothing else remains. The wind hums through the grass, the flowers don their bright summer colors, and the leaves cover the trees and earth with beautiful foliage in the fall, but the era is long gone. The roadbed has gone back to squirrels, a few hikers, and an occasional bear.

Thanks to the ingenuity of L. L. Nunn and the determination of Otto Mears, Telluride turned the corner of the early 1890s and headed into the final decade of the nineteenth century with the kind of fervor that would give the Gay Nineties their name.

What more could a town ask for? The mountains

were filled with rich ore, electricity could power the mines forever, and now there was transportation to get the wealth to the market. The population reached five thousand, prospects were unlimited, and, as always in times of prosperity, the end was nowhere in sight.

People came to the area from everywhere. America was a melting pot, and Telluride set a proud example. At the New Sheridan Hotel and the Cosmopolitan one could order fine French cooking and receive excellent continental service from Jean Pomateau and Frank Maumee. The "Up-to Date-Outfitter," W. B. Van Atta, a gentile, offered a complete stock of clothing for men and women, along with a fine assortment of yard goods. Rittmaster, a Jew, and Connor, an Irishman, sold women's wear and varieties. Floatens, a Dane, ran a general dry goods store, and there were two Chinese laundries. Germans did the boardinghouse cooking, and a German named Hilgenhouse ran a grocery. Most

Photograph by Richard L. Fetter

"Nothing else remains . . . the era is long gone"

Courtesy of San Miguel County Museum

Telluride newspaper ad in '90s
— vintage prices and vintage
wines in the gastronomic days
of Pomateau and Maumee.

Courtesy of San Miguel County Museum

Telluride had more than a hundred saloonkeepers and gamblers, most of them
American. The games were fairly run, and owners of gambling houses had credit at
the banks on an equal footing with merchants.

Courtesy of San Miguel County Museum

Advertisement for Van Atta's

Courtesy of San Miguel County Museum

W. B. Van Atta's, the "Up-to-date-Outfitter" of the '90s

of the more than one hundred gamblers and saloon-keepers in town were Americans. No one ever minded the normal gambling percentage in favor of the house, and most people felt the games were fairly run. In fact, practically every operator enjoyed good standing in the community and credit with the banks on an equal footing with the merchants.

It didn't take long for the Sheridan cuisine to become well known throughout Colorado. The menu offered vichyssoise and fresh strawberries, possum, pork tenderloin, seafood, and a plank steak that was two inches thick, a foot wide, and two feet long. The gastronomic delights were complemented with an extensive selection of California and European wines and, if a man wished, an assortment of vintage cigars. To dine better, most people agreed, one had to go to the Brown Palace in Denver; otherwise there was no place that

Courtesy of San Miguel County Museum

No one minded the normal gambling percentage in favor of the house. Operators enjoyed good standing in the community.

could compare. At Christmas the Sheridan and other Telluride bars offered bowls of steaming Tom and Jerries for those who were ready to come in out of the cold and enjoy some civilized living.

It was a man's world however. Women were still twenty years away from having the right to vote. In those days the unwritten rule at the Sheridan dictated that a lady enter through the side service door and remain in a waiting parlour until the gentleman was ready to dine. Otherwise the rules were posted for all to observe:

Don't shoot the pianist, he's doing his damndest.
Please don't swear, damn you.
Beds 50¢, with sheets 75¢.
No horses above first floor.
No more than 5 in a bed.
Warmth provided by horse blankets, liquor, Christian zeal.
Funerals on the house.

Courtesy of San Miguel County Museum

"Roulette pays"

Saloons grew everywhere, homes were built, dance halls thrived, and "the line" down on Pacific Avenue prospered as never before. Yet this rollicking, wide-open mining town that had begun "to put on airs" a decade earlier maintained all efforts to keep its image right and proper.

In an often-quoted but never authenticated letter, a lady in Boston wrote in 1891 to one of the Telluride town officials to inquire about the town and the state of its society since she was interested in taking her two children there to live for the sake of their health. She received the following reply:

. . . As for sowciety it is bang up. This is a mighty morrel town, considern' that theres 69 saloons and two newspapers to a pop-pylatin of 1247. But every saloon has a sine up sayin "All fitin must be done outside. No kilin in this room." Only two men has been killed since Monday, and termorroer will be Wednesday. Cheatin' at gamblin is punished by linchin, and every effort is bein made to put the town on a morrel basis equal to Rico. Ladies is universally respected and I sell them beer at half price when they buy at my place. There is a grand sacred concert and free dance every Sunday that the preacher dont stay ter home on ac-count of the big rush at this bowlin alley. Dont hezzytate about comin here on account of sowciety. This is a morrel town.

She decided not to come.

The lady would have found much of the town to her liking. North of the main street was the abode of the "respectable" element. Women didn't drink or smoke and were highly respected. No woman hesitated to walk past the saloons and gambling places near the stores where they shopped, and they held their little "at homes" once a month to receive guests and enter-tain friends. All was very formal for evening get-togethers whether the occasion be the theater, the cir-cus, or one of the many good traveling shows that passed through.

In the winter they went skating or tobogganing. Ski-ing was strictly functional, a means by which the miners who were Scandinavian traveled to and from the mines. Skis were boards fashioned at home; bindings consisted of a leather strap over the boot tops. One of the exciting pastimes was to take a big shovel, sit on it with the handle between your legs, and slide down a slope recently bowled out by an avalanche. The seat was too hot to touch by the time you reached the bottom of the ride.

"Society" had a definite Anglo-Saxon nature. Much of the financing came from the East, and there were several Londoners and Australians who made up the bulk of the engineers, managers, and — along with New Englanders and New Yorkers — the financiers.

The proper northside ladies never crossed to the seamy south. Here life was wide open. Along Pacific Avenue life raced on, colorful and unchecked, at the Senate, Pick and Gad, White House, Big Swede, Swede-Finn Hall, Silver Bell, Monte Carlo, Midway,

Photograph by Richard L. Fetter

The Pick and Gad, in its day, was one of the thriving houses on the south side of town.

Belmont, Gold Belt, Idle Hour, and the other twenty-six bars and houses of "the line" with their bar and dance hall downstairs and series of rooms upstairs. Most girls worked out of cribs, two-room structures which lined Pacific Avenue. On the south side also lived the tough Scandinavian and Cornish workers. Stud poker, roulette, faro, fan-tan, twenty-one, seven and a half, hokey-pokey, and all the banking games went on all hours of the day and night. The atmosphere was carnival-like. Saloons sported a free lunch counter if you bought a 5-cent beer. The Corner Saloon offered possum as a specialty for the Southerners. Lights burned brightly along the street, and the men were welcomed everywhere. There were no inhibitions; men did pretty well as they pleased. It wasn't exactly Boston.

Then again, in Boston a man had local taxes to pay. In Telluride a citizen was relieved of this annoying aspect of life by the fact that prostitution on Pacific Avenue not only existed but thrived. There was no doubt that prostitution was a firmly entrenched institution. It had always been there and probably always would be. So why not tax it? The madams couldn't have cared less. Each one was charged $150 a week, which hardly dented the profits. Upon payment they were allowed to continue in business, and the total collected was enough to keep the city operating profitably. There was a popular theory that prostitution in an area where men outnumbered women four to one allowed decent women to walk the streets safely. It wasn't that the citizens bought the argument; the economic soundness of the approach to the problem simply had undeniable merits.

Girls weren't exactly running into Telluride from all over the territory, and turnover in the dance halls was great. This prompted the town to hire a woman who traveled across the United States soliciting entertainers. The majority of recruits arrived broke and stayed only long enough to earn money to get back home. The girls worked on a percentage basis, getting chits from the bartender for every drink bought for them. Some of the girls were possibly drugged or gotten drunk to get them to Telluride; others came thinking they would get jobs as bookkeepers or in other respectable capacities.

Those who were there in those days recall that it was always a dramatic, sad day when one of the dance hall girls died. The funeral would be organized by her "sisters," and whether the streets were dry or full of mud or snow, the girls went to church for the service. Afterwards they followed the hearse up the main street wearing their gaudy dresses and high-heeled shoes. Perhaps the band from the dance hall would play a dirge. Following the burial, business went on as usual.

Photograph by Richard L. Fetter

The Senate, once the house of kindly "Big Billy" and the employer of a young fellow named Jack Dempsey, is open today as a popular place restored in the old style. Next door was the Silver Bell.

Feelings were equally profound and sincere when one of the miners died.

Of all the bordellos and the twenty-six saloons in town and the more than one hundred girls who worked the line, no place was more popular than the Senate, run by a popular madam known as "Big Billy." She was the kind-hearted woman who never turned anyone out into the cold, the classic madam who cared for the sick and was held in high esteem by the northside crowd. During her day the Senate was a boisterous place where a sheriff got an ear shot off and a man shot his friend after the two had spent two nights drinking together. The Senate kitchen was also where a young man named Jack Dempsey from Manassa, Colorado, worked for a time washing dishes before he decided boxing might provide a more lucrative living. The 1880 wooden bar, brass rail spittoons, and Victorian parlor setting, all in use once again today, were the scene of many a card game and fight, and many a night when a man forgot the hard life he was leading and spent all his hard-earned money.

There was at the same time, however, a strong civic-minded nature to the town which was just as noticeable as in the early '80s when it was "putting on airs." The great increase in the population had brought the number of school-age children to 212. Of these, 173 were enrolled in 1893. Average attendance was 95, the discrepancy in numbers being due to the absence of many families during the winter. The teaching staff had been expanded to three, a principalship had been established, and the school was so crowded that the primary section was on half-day sessions. Even with the addition of extra classrooms in 1892 and 1894, it was clear that the old schoolhouse of 1883 would no longer suffice.

Plans for a new school were undertaken, and a new

building was completed in 1895. Due to faulty brick, it collapsed almost immediately. By the following year a good school was ready for use, thanks to the raising of $29,000 to reconstruct the building. Even at the height of good times, the people never overlooked the importance of education during their quest for wealth. In addition to the school in Telluride, there were also schools at the Tomboy, the Liberty Bell, Smuggler, Pandora, and Alta mines, plus two on Wilson Mesa, two on Hastings Mesa, three at Sawpit, and two at Placerville.

The '90s also saw the raising of money for an opera house and two new churches. After existing as the mission of Ouray, St. Patrick's Church was organized in 1896 at a cost of $4,800. Under the guidance of the energetic and popular Father O'Rourke, membership reached two hundred by 1899. In 1897 the Methodist Church was built in Telluride after much hard work and quick thinking by Bishop Warren.

The Bishop went on one fund-raising journey with Mr. L. L. Kinikin, a respected citizen of the town, to the office of John Herron, manager of the Tomboy Mining Company. When Kinikin introduced the two men, Herron asked Bishop Warren if he was related to a preacher named Warren in Boston. The bishop acknowledged that they were brothers. Herron went on to say that he had sat under the ministry of the Boston Warren many times, and that he was born of a missionary mother. Since coming west however, Herron said he had become "somewhat rusty."

"Mr. Herron," the bishop replied, "the gold in the Tomboy Mine has been there hundreds of years but has not grown rusty." Stumped and impressed, Herron gave Bishop Warren a check for $500, and, soon after, a $10,000 church was built a block north of the Sheridan.

Religious men continued to be interesting, hearty individuals who worked hard in behalf of their beliefs.

One of the most popular and unconventional of these was the Reverend Mr. Bradley, who came every Sunday evening and preached from newspaper stories rather than the Bible. Not surprisingly, his most successful night was when he announced the topic would be gambling. The room was packed, and the miners filled the collection plate afterwards with piles of gold coins.

It was also during the '90s that the town band graduated from a group of enthusiasts who snowshoed to Rico to a fine organization that went to Denver as the Telluride Cornet Band and won first prize three consecutive years in "The Festival of the Mountain and Plain."

The leader of the band was big Jim Knous, uncle of the governor of Colorado. Jim, a towering man who approached seven feet in height with his headgear on, cut a colorful, flashing figure marching down the main street with his flourishing baton and tall black shako with a bright red plume. For a time Jim served as the town marshall. At 6 feet 5 inches and 285 pounds, he was enough of a man to do the job. Possible breaches of the peace were often settled by bumping a few heads together and sending the boys home. Breaking up trouble rather than making arrests didn't do much for the town treasury, however, and the City Council fired him from his post. After all, it was enough to ask a musician to keep the peace without adding revenue responsibilities as well.

Keeping the law wasn't always easy in Telluride; several peace officers died violent deaths. One of the most controversial officers was the brutal Jim Clark. Clark was someone whose total dedication to the law was questionable. There was a strong suspicion that many of his absences from Telluride were due to jobs that he pulled with a gang of men in the vicinity. He was a crack shot, acquired a lot of enemies over the years, and kept a Winchester in each of four stores in town, as well as two guns on himself. There were many who said that Clark helped many poor families with the results of his unexplained activities, but the city council feared him, fired him, and asked him to leave town. Clark refused to go.

There is no certain proof that the council was behind the murder, but one day in 1895 Clark walked out of the Brunswick Saloon on the corner of Spruce and Colorado and was shot by a gunman on top of the San Juan Saloon. The bullet tore into Clark's chest, and he staggered across the street to one of the cribs on "the line." Within fifty minutes he was dead.

One of Clark's successors, Art Gigline, was also murdered, but there was no question about who fired the shot. Jess Munn, a miner working in the Pennsylvania, had a girl who lived in one of the cribs on Pacific

Photograph by Suzanne C. Fetter

"The cribs" today. In 1895 controversial peace officer Jim Clark died here after being ambushed by a gunman on top of the San Juan saloon.

Avenue. Gigline had been seeing the girl, and Munn threatened him that he had better stop. Gigline took Munn's gun away and went to see the girl. Later Munn, armed with another gun, found the two of them in the Cozy Korner. An argument arose, and the marshall and the girl walked out with Munn behind them, waving his gun and shouting at Gigline, "You'll never take another gun from me!"

Munn then fired four times, and Gigline died immediately. His killer ran to the livery barn, grabbed a horse, and rode to Ophir, where he abandoned the horse. Eventually he was found in New Mexico, brought to trial, and convicted of murder. Munn died soon after, killed in an attempt to escape from the Canon City Prison.

Recourse to a gun was frequent, but consequences weren't always lethal. At one point there was a judge named Wescott who had a running feud with a fellow by the name of Avery. Avery would get drunk, stand in the doorway of his cabin, and riddle the judge's place with Winchester bullets. Wescott would hide under his bed unless he, too, were drunk, in which case he would load his eight-gauge shotgun with nails, stove bolts, and whatever else he could find, and blaze away. The two lived 150 feet from each other, but since their aims weren't very good no one took the feud seriously. Wescott's arm and shoulder would get sore and bruised from the recoil of the shotgun. The only honest wound came to Avery when a lucky shot sent a stove bolt through his pants into his bottom. Neighbors yanked it out with an old bullet mould used to pull porcupine quills out of dog's noses.

The sharpshooting judge also provided a little wintertime merriment when he got himself snowed in at one of the mines and became so hungry he ate the bottom of his chair, made of woven strips of untanned deer hide.

One of the more interesting men in the valley during those days was Lon Remine, who, with his brother Bill, had been prospecting in the valley for more than a year when Fallon arrived in 1874. In fact, one of Webb's parties out of Wisconsin reported running into the Remines on their first trip up the valley in '81. With a sweeping gesture the Remines told the newcomers they owned all the land in the area, but the bluff was called and the newcomers went on to Columbia.

Lon Remine was a loner who lived in a cave for a while and then in a rundown shack, but he was a well-liked man. When he finally struck it rich after nearly twenty years of prospecting around the area, the Tel-

Courtesy of Homer Reid Collection

This barn on Hastings Mesa, one of the most photographed barns in Colorado, stands not far from the house built by Lon Remine after he struck it rich.

luride *Journal* wrote, "Everyone who had not already heard that Lon Remine has struck it, will be pleased to read this item. He has got five feet of yellow copper, iron and lime, carrying galena that runs over twenty dollars. He has hardly got the vein in place yet, and it is liable to be better in the next twenty feet drifting. His location is most favorably situated for working, as it is so far below timberline that the magpies have to climb the hill to find a place to roost. We hope and believe that Lon has got a bonanza and that loneliness, privation, and toil have for once been rewarded."

Remine and his partner sold out for $40,000, and the lifelong prospector ordered a fine new home built east of the creek on Hastings Mesa that bears his name. Upon completion of the house, he went back to Kentucky, where he had been born in 1845, and sought to bring back his bride. When the girl wanted to bring her mother along, Remine objected and returned to Telluride alone.

Lon Remine's hospitality became legendary. A tin cup was hung to the side of his door by the liquor barrel for those who were thirsty. Two generations of children came to play on the bench out in front and listen to his drawled stories of prospecting and hunting. In a sensitive, nostalgic composition for her high school English class, Mabel G. March wrote in 1931 of her childhood days at the house of this man whose hair hung in a tangled mass almost to his shoulders. She recalled how his "cabin" was furnished with stuff from the city dump, and how the tall, angular, slightly stooped figure would go to the dump to pick out his clothes. His usual garb was a frayed rusty blue serge coat and dirty overalls. He tied his shoes with twine and wore a black hat. When Remine came to her house for dinner, no one could eat except her father because the grimy guest's hands would leave smudge marks on the glassware and dishes. The kids would always go to his place with fresh bread or pie that their mothers had baked, and they never returned empty-handed. He'd give them peas from his garden or treat them to some of the wild berry jelly that he made. In the spring he would invite them to come and pick crocuses.

Perhaps it was due to his lonely family life that Lon Remine was so warm and hospitable to the kids who came to see him. Not only did he leave the girl he would have married in Kentucky, but he and his brother Bill were so far apart as individuals that they fought on different sides in the Civil War. Throughout their lives they never reconciled. When Bill was sick and dying, Lon sent food with instructions not to say where it came from lest his brother reject it. Lon finally died in 1929, alone and unattended. The people of Telluride buried him next to his brother in Lone Tree Cemetery, where a marker signifies that these two adversaries were among the earliest white men to prospect and settle in the San Miguel Valley.

For the man who didn't want to take the risks of prospecting, the '90s offered the chance for steady, if hard, employment. Except for a time during the recession of 1893, a man could expect to find work at one of the mines as a mucker or common laborer that would bring him $3 a day. Good machine men could make $4 a day, and a superintendent could earn $300 a month. For a $1-a-day fee there was ample food and adequate lodging in a boardinghouse.

The boardinghouse dining hall was a place for eating and little else. The hall was fitted with long tables with one end against the wall. All along the top of the table was a shelf fourteen inches high, upon which food was placed. The men were let in, they sat down, and food was piled on their plates. When they finished, they left.

Life may have been tough, but the moral code was

simple. A man could drink and get stone drunk; it didn't matter. He could go broke, and somebody would give him money to get a meal or get back to the mine. But let him lie or cheat or steal, and there wouldn't be much more time for that fellow. Any breach of faith made you a marked man. Will Webb had noticed the same code existing in the '80s. A man in the mountains could break into a cabin and fix himself a meal, but if he stole something it was grounds for murder.

There wasn't much chance for a miner to enjoy himself. Hours were long, and days off were few and far between. Christmas and the Fourth of July were the only official holidays. Men put in a seven-day week at the mine; their only vacation was a voluntary lay-off when they felt the need.

Upon receiving his month's salary, a miner might drop into Van Atta's, buy a new suit for $15 or $20, get a new shirt, underwear, shoes, and a hat. Van Atta would throw in a necktie and suspenders. The next stop would be Harry Miller's barbershop. Here he'd have a shave, shine, massage, shampoo, and a bath. Harry had six bathtubs in cubicles in the back of the shop, and for $5 one could become a new man. Then perhaps a few drinks, a little poker, and supper. By midnight he probably wouldn't know where he was and would be happily covered with mud, tobacco juice and whiskey. If he had spent all his money, good old Mr. Van Atta could be counted on to give him $2 to rent a horse and get back to the mine for another month or two. One fellow from the Tomboy came down from the mine after what he called a fourteen-month winter; after ten days in town he went back to work flat broke.

They say there were also a few who lived quietly, read good books, saved their money, and went on to establish businesses elsewhere.

There was a lot of respect for strength in the mining camps and a lot of belief in strength as the great human

Telluride Hose Team No. 1. The champion: 100 yards Wet Test in Southwestern Colorado, July 3, 1892. The First National Bank is now the BPOE Lodge in Telluride.

equalizer in the struggle against the powers of nature. Drill contests were tremendously popular among the hammer strikers and drill turners. The contests were held on the Fourth of July as part of the annual celebrations. It was a day on which thousands of dollars changed hands.

The day began with a blast of powder that was enough to knock anyone out of bed who wasn't up already. There were parades in the morning with brass bands, marching miners, fire engines all decked out in crepe paper, fraternal orders in uniform, and princesses on wagons decorated with evergreens and columbines.

Dogs and firecrackers were everywhere. David Lavender recalls that "Everywhere was the unabashed ripple of muscle."

A ten-ton block of granite was set on a platform in the middle of Colorado Avenue for the drillers. The object was to see who could punch the deepest hole in the granite within a certain time, and there was a lot of competition between the mines. Practice began months ahead of time, a few hours per week being spent in fifteen-minute periods drilling away at the hardest slabs in the mountains. Men worked in pairs, one striking the drill for three to five minutes, the other turning the drill. The turner had to be good, for if the drill became stuck in the rock there was no chance to win. The drill had to be properly tempered and the blows struck with respect for the power of the drill. Blows were struck with amazing skill and speed. A good pair, alternating frequently, could bore into the hardest granite at an inch and a half a minute. The Reverend Mr. Gibbons, passing through Telluride in the late '80s, noted that "Twenty-five inches or more have been drilled into the granite in a quarter of an hour, something which our fathers thought never could be accomplished by the hand of man."

There was something for everyone — tugs-of-war, hose teams blasting each other with water, horse races, and a baseball game. One of the popular events was the hose-cart race when teams of men would strap themselves into traces and strain through a course lined by cheering crowds that placed heavy bets on the outcome. In 1892, when Telluride's top team beat Durango, supporters charted a special train on the Southern to go to the race.

In many ways the basic honesty in the town and the standards of life there were much to be recommended as Telluride grew in the '90s. There were many instances in the gossip column of the *Journal* such as the one of August 14, 1896, that said, "W. M. Bramhall, proprietor of the City Drug Store, has returned home from the East and is more than pleased to again breathe the pure mountain air of Telluride." Two years earlier, in June 1894, the wife of L. L. Kinikin went back to Sedalia, Missouri, for a two-months' visit but wrote to him after three weeks to say she hadn't seen the sun

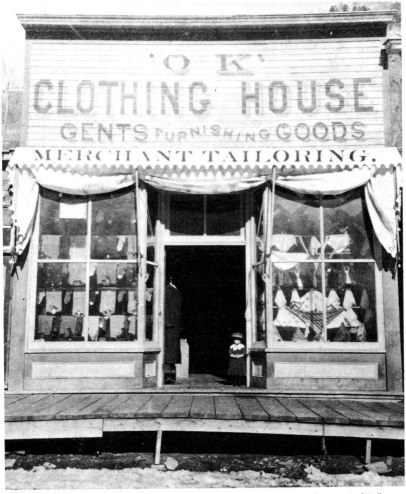

The "O.K. Clothing House" in the late '80s

since she left Colorado and that she felt she was too far from the sky. She was coming home right away.

On the very last day of the nineteenth century, the *Journal* stated:

Telluride is as quiet, peaceful, orderly, self-contained a community as can be found in the United States. It has never had a lynching; mob law has never usurped court and peace-keeping responsibilities. Only a few murders have been committed. It has high grade schools, ample churches, and numerous social, literary and benevolent orders.

The same edition of the *Journal* found, rather surprisingly, that stock raising and agriculture were no

A shoe shop in Telluride's main street in prosperous days

less important than mining and that a large "and very desirable proportion of citizens find employment in these vocations."

Telluride was changing with the approach of the twentieth century. A further indication was the attempt on February 3, 1900, to close down the gambling houses. Proprietors of two leading saloons were arrested. Most prominent people opposed the action, believing the saloons wouldn't stay closed long — which they didn't. The same thing had been tried in Ouray, Silverton, and other mining towns with equal lack of success.

Yet there was a change in the air. It proved to be not one of morality or life style but a gentle change in the wind of fortune. Had Telluride known what the next half century would bring, the people would very likely have been content to quietly leave their calendars forever at 1899.

II. THE TOWN WITHOUT A BELLYACHE

In 1947 the postmaster of Zermatt, Switzerland, wrote a brief history of his famous mountain village in which he said that towns, like people, have their ups and downs, their moments of prosperity and ruin. To this, Telluride can only nod quietly in agreement.

If in the nineteenth century Fortune was content to smile coyly at one and turn a cold shoulder to another, in the first half of the twentieth century she turned away from the area with rude abruptness, leaving a path of blood and ruin behind her.

Courtesy of Homer Reid Collection

An early 1920s outing

New Year's resolutions and high hopes for a brand new century were hardly a year old when gunfire broke out at the Smuggler-Union Mine. Four men lay dead, and another five or six were wounded. The problem was not one of personal differences among miners but in the very system under which the men worked. In 1899 the "fathom" or "contract" system of labor had been introduced in the Smuggler-Union. Under this system a miner's wages were based on the number of fathoms he could work a day, rather than on the fixed wage system which was typical of the area. A fathom was six feet high, six feet long, and as wide as the vein the man was working. If a miner worked a wide vein his earnings were small. Thus, many miners found they were working longer than eight hours a day and still earning less than the accepted $3-a-day wage. In fact, some men found themselves in debt, having accumulated expenses for powder, room, and board greater than their wages. Nor did the miners have a voice in their contract. Management offered a steadily decreasing price per fathom which the miner could accept or reject but not otherwise alter. At first management required that the miner only break the ore, but later it required that he break it into suitable size and throw it into mill holes.

Millionaires were walking around outside the mines in fine clothes and driving handsome horses, but it was the men inside who made it possible, and their working conditions were far from ideal. Even under the normal system, $3 for an eight-hour day was the maximum a miner could expect. Outside laborers earned $2.50 for a ten-hour day and mill men made $4 for a twelve-hour day. The work was hard, and accidents were frequent. One of the more unusual occurrences was the electrocution of a Greek when he took hold of a trolley cable used by electric locomotives going to and from the Alta Mine. His body hung from the line in a crouching position and had to be knocked down with a pole.

Of more daily concern at the Alta was the method of processing amalgam, a mixture of gold and mercury. Due to inefficiencies in the system, men could and did get mercury poisoning. They sometimes lost teeth and died young because of it. This was only one of the hazards of working in that particular mine in a day when safety was an unknown concept, and fires, cave-ins, slides, and personal accidents were commonplace.

The introduction of the fathom system at the Smuggler-Union proved to be the straw that broke the camel's back. On May 2, 1901, the miners at the Smug-

Courtesy of Homer Reid Collection

$2.50 for a 10-hour day

gler went on strike. The mine closed for six weeks, finally reopening with nonunion labor. The new laborers went to work not under the fathom system but by the day, at the regular wages of the district. Arthur Collins, manager of the mine, who had originally introduced the fathom system, was in effect hiring men to work at the Smuggler under conditions which the striking men were trying to obtain. Naturally the miners were furious. They sent delegations to management in search of compromise and attempted to induce scabs to stay away; they were unsuccessful in both cases.

During the night of July 3, some 250 miners armed with rifles, shotguns, and revolvers hid in positions around the mine. At dawn they confronted the night shift of scabs. They told the men that if they quit work immediately they wouldn't be harmed. Otherwise, there was going to be trouble. A barrage of shots answered from inside the shaft of the Smuggler, and one of the union men fell dead. Union men then opened fire at the buildings and held the scabs at bay until they capitulated several hours later. Three of the men inside the mine lay dead; another five or six were wounded.

The nonunion men had surrendered with the understanding that they would be allowed to leave town unharmed. Those who had not managed to sneak away were lined up and marched out of town toward Ouray County. The miners didn't totally abide by their word. Several captives were beaten and one was shot through both arms. The incident later boomeranged, setting the precedent for the deportation and abuse of union men by management forces in the labor dispute that followed two years later.

A truce was patched up between the union and the company later in the day. Eventually a commission helped produce an agreement granting the miners the $3 wage for an eight-hour day. The miners returned to

At the Alta, mercury poisoning, resulting in loss of teeth and even death, was a turn-of-the-century hazard that fueled the crises at the mines.

work. Soldiers, who had been mobilized in Denver when news of the violence first spread, were relieved from duty. But the worst was still to come.

In November a load of hay at the entrance of the mine caught fire. Flames and smoke were sucked into the tunnel, endangering the men inside. Instead of immediately blowing up the mouth of the tunnel and warning the men to use other exits, efforts were made to remove nearby firearms. Inside, men who had just gone to work were caught by the heat and smoke being sucked into the tunnel. Thorwald Torkelson, the shift boss, and Carey Barkly rushed into the tunnel to warn men to get out, closing the tunnel mouth as they went in. Meeting a couple of trammers on the way, they ordered them to unhitch and run for their lives. Each man unhooked his load, grabbed the tail of his animal and slapped hard, urging it towards the entrance. The horse in the lead burst through the tunnel door and pulled his driver to safety. The other horse was overcome by fumes and fell dead before reaching the opening. The driver finally escaped in the other direction.

The fire steadily worsened, and the foreman from the nearby Tomboy Mine ordered the tunnel dynamited — but it was too late. Men had been asphyxiated by smoke; others were killed in the explosion as they tried to find a way out the main entrance. Those who had rushed in to warn the others were among those who perished. The tunnel was ruined, the boardinghouse burned, and twenty-eight men died. The miners charged that Manager Collins had been negligent in putting out the fire and in not having safety doors installed to protect the mine.

No action was taken by the mine owners, and tempers remained high. When a great natural disaster occurred later that same winter, each side was quick to find fault with the other. Great snowslides tore down the mountainsides, destroying the boarding and bunkhouses of the Liberty Bell Mine. In four separate avalanches eighteen men were killed. Angry miners claimed the slides were caused by the removal of timber from avalanche slopes for use at the mines. Adjutant General Gardner of the National Guard thought differently. "I cannot but believe," he exclaimed, "that the recent series of disasters are the judgment of Almighty God upon the crimes that have been committed in that camp in the name of labor, and I am not a religious fanatic, either."

Whatever the cause of the disaster, or whether or not there was any human fault, the Liberty Bell snowslide of 1902 was one of the worst disasters in the town's history. The first slide roared down the moun-

tain early in the morning of February 28, carrying off
not just the boarding and bunkhouses but the tramway
station and ore-loading house as well. L. M. Umstead,
who worked near the crusher with his pack mules, had
just come from breakfast and was in the stable saddling
his animals when he heard a thunderous noise. Suddenly the stable became pitch black, and he stepped
outside to find all had become dark. The air was filled
with flying snow.

Thinking it was a great gust of wind, he slammed
the stable door shut, waited a few seconds, then peered
through a crack. As it grew light again he opened the
door and saw the tram cable swinging about and buck-
ets rolling down the hill. He stepped outside and
looked toward the boardinghouse, but nothing was
there. Down the slope was a scattering of timber and
boards sticking out of slabs and chunks of snow. Several lives were lost under the crushing tons of snow
that levelled everything before it. A search party went
out and was completely caught by a second avalanche.
Despite the danger of further slides, a third party went
out the following day. Another avalanche came down,
this one blocking the trail before the bodies of the men
already lost could be reached. The men turned back to
town without the dead or injured men at the mine. A
full day passed before they were able to get back and
break a trail through the snow.

In the Sheridan a Cornish miner was relaxing over a
beer when news of the slides reached him. He set out
to help the rescuers and was overrun by a avalanche.
His body was found months later at the bottom of a
drift. Telluride was shocked. Businesses closed for the
day when the funerals were held. The town turned out
nearly to a man and followed the bodies to the cemetery. For some time men forgot their differences, and
the months passed in relative peace.

The respite from trouble at the mines only meant

death had moved into town. On October 29, 1902, a dance-hall girl named Mary Nash was senselessly murdered in a bar. She and four men had been playing cards when a quarrel developed over fifty cents. The bartender settled the dispute, the game broke up, and one of the men angrily left the table and stalked to a stove in the corner of the room. The woman called to him to rejoin the game, and in answer he opened fire on her. She staggered across the room and fell dead. The murderer and his companions covered the rest of the people in the bar with revolvers and backed out of the dance hall, warning that the first person to move would be shot down too. The man's three companions were later apprehended, but he escaped into the hills.

Times were such that a murderer didn't always have to disappear. A bartender named Umstead had a quarrel with a cattleman, a tinhorn gambler named Fred Leaning, who was called "just plain mean" by people who knew him. Umstead, undaunted, took two revolvers and went to get his man. They met in the Tremont, a saloon that stood next to the bank Cassidy's gang had robbed on the main street. Leaning shot Umstead in the back. As he rolled a cigarette he snapped, "Nobody can threaten me with a gun and get away with it." At the trial he plead self-defense on the grounds that Umstead was "looking for him." He was acquitted, despite having shot the man in the back.

In November labor-management relations were suddenly pushed to the breaking point when Manager Collins of the Smuggler placed advertisements in all the local papers offering work at his mine for any of the men on a list of scabs he had received. The next night he was shot in the back by a shotgun fired through a window of the company office at the Pandora, where he had been working late. He died a few days later at the Miners' Union Hospital. Several men were indicted, but no conclusive proof of guilt was ever found.

After the death of Collins, Colonel Livermore put his son-in-law, Bulkeley Wells, in charge of the Smuggler-Union. The new manager was as glamorous and intriguing a man as any who ever lived in Telluride. Smooth, educated, well-dressed, and possessing a certain flair, he cut a striking figure in the town. Wells arrived in Telluride as the result of a card game in a New York City men's club where he met Harry Payne Whitney. He was invited to play and joined the game believing that the stakes were $1 a point when actually they were $10. He played casually through the evening and won 160 points for a total of, to his surprise, $1,600. Whitney was impressed that anyone could play for such stakes with Wells' coolness, unaware that Wells had misunderstood the amount. Whitney spoke with him after the game and learned that Wells had a mining background. Convinced that anyone who could play cards like that had what it took to gamble and win bigger stakes elsewhere, Whitney went on to authorize Wells' eventual investment of millions of dollars in mining ventures in the West.

On the Fourth of July, 1903, the new Smuggler manager joined the rest of the town to listen to presidential candidate William Jennings Bryan, who delivered his famous Cross of Gold speech from a bunting-clad platform in front of the Sheridan Hotel. For a time attention was directed to the national issue of whether the country should go permanently on a standard of gold or a combination of gold and silver. Bryan spoke strongly in favor of a bimetal standard, but he was arguing a losing cause. Unfortunately for Telluride, hopes for peace in the coming days were no more likely to be realized than Bryan's dream.

Later in the summer, miners in Cripple Creek went on strike for an eight-hour day. Telluride miners went on a sympathy strike, since the two places were then the centers of the mining industry in Colorado. The

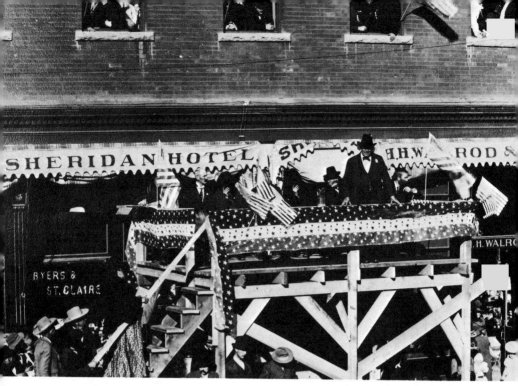

Courtesy of Homer Reid Collection

William Jennings Bryan delivering his Cross of Gold speech in front of the Sheridan. To this day no one in Telluride knows why the two gentlemen to the left of Bryan seem to be hiding their faces with their hats.

strike began at the mills on September 1, when the men demanded a reduction from a twelve- to an eight-hour day. It spread to the mines on October 31, when about one hundred miners at the Tomboy went on a sympathy walkout because the manager had reopened the mill with nonunion men.

The *Telluride Journal* sided with the mine owners, and it was boycotted. Businesses and saloons that failed to display a "fair" card in their windows met the same fate. Tempers grew short, and skirmishes occurred. Hired gunmen from as far away as Wyoming suddenly began to appear on the streets.

On November 5, members of the San Juan District Owner's Association, which had been organized in August by Bulkeley Wells, requested Governor Peabody to send troops from Colorado's National Guard so management could reopen the mines with nonunion men. Meanwhile, the miners took over the Smuggler-Union and wired the governor that "The miners is in peaceable possession of the Smuggler-Union properties."

The assassination of Collins in 1902 had prejudiced the governor against the labor union in Telluride, and he agreed to send two troops of cavalry and six companies of infantry, about five hundred men and officers. Late in the afternoon of the 24th a train hauled by two steam engines brought the first contingent of the National Guard to Telluride. The lead engine pushed a gondola full of soldiers ahead of the train. Bales of hay were stacked on the sides of the car with portholes between them for guns. A trainsman was posted in the front end of the car to give signals to the engine crew in case the train was attacked. Most of the soldiers were young kids, and they breathed a great sigh when the train arrived without incident.

Courtesy of San Miguel County Museum

Runnels, a hired gunman

Upon the arrival of the troops, nonunion scabs were brought in to replace the strikers. The men were by and large Greeks, Austrians, Swedes, and Finns brought in especially for that purpose and put up at Redman's Opera House. Many of the miners, particularly the leaders, were kicked out of town. Fort Peabody was erected at the top of Imogene Pass to prevent union sympathizers from sneaking over from Ouray and Silverton to aid the miners. The red light district was padlocked, and gambling was suspended. To hold any kind of meeting it was necessary to get a permit from the sergeant of the National Guard.

In addition to these regulations and actions, Wells organized a local company of the National Guard with headquarters at the Stubbs and Jakeway Opera House. Wells was the captain and trained a corps of men that

Courtesy of Homer Reid Collection

In 1903 the stores still looked prosperous, but the militia was needed to keep the peace.

Courtesy of Homer Reid Collection

Fort Peabody on top of Imogene Pass, the highest military fort in the United States, was erected to keep Union sympathizers from sneaking over from Ouray and Silverton to aid the miners.

consisted mainly of cowboys and Spanish-American War veterans. Along with John Herron, manager of the Tomboy, Wells also formed a Citizen's Alliance that was organized to watch out for the interests of management.

Wells, active and outspoken in the management cause, became the target of an assassination attempt that should have blown him to pieces. A unionist by the name of Adams managed to place a bomb under Wells' bed. It exploded in the middle of the night and blew the Smuggler-Union manager out of his bedroom. Wells miraculously escaped the explosion uninjured, although its force was sufficient to imbed his pistol in the wainscot ceiling of the front porch. Adams was soon caught. An ugly atmosphere was developing when Wells arrived on the scene and prevented what would have been a certain lynching.

"Boys, don't do it," he said. "If we get one legal conviction our troubles with the union are over. If we make one illegal move, our name is mud!"

The men consented, but Adams wasn't convicted. A clever lawyer obtained a change of venue to an agricultural county where a jury wanted no part of Telluride's problems and released him. From there, Adams and Telluride parted ways.

Six days after the arrival of the militia, forty alleged troublesome strikers were rounded up, convicted of vagrancy, and deported to Montrose. By December 31 the determined efforts of the owners had resulted in every mill in the district being partially opened, over the strenuous objection of the Western Federation of Miners.

Life was just beginning to get back to normal when martial law was suddenly declared on January 4, 1904. People were prohibited from going onto the streets after 8 P.M. Even the paper boys had to obtain a pass to sell their papers from 8 until midnight. Military authorities required passes to travel over roads and trails in the district, and all firearms were ordered to be registered and turned in.

By February 2 a total of eighty-three men had been deported from Telluride. Any union worker who stirred up any kind of trouble would soon find himself out of the county, often accompanied by the militia as far as Ridgway on the Rio Grande Southern.

On February 21 Major Hill, who had been in command of the troops since their arrival, was replaced by Capt. Bulkeley Wells. Within three weeks, Governor Peabody, believing order had been restored, suspended martial law and recalled the militia. The action proved to be premature.

As soon as the militia left, the Citizens' Alliance met, armed themselves, searched the town, and rounded up about sixty union men and sympathizers. The men were put on a train at 1:30 A.M. and told not to come back. Upon learning this, other Telluride citizens and officials requested that the National Guard be sent once again to protect life and property. On March 11, three hundred infantrymen returned to town, and martial law was reinstated.

When the district judge ruled that the deported miners should be allowed to return to Telluride, most of the men decided to return en masse in a special train. The National Guard and Citizen's Alliance, both under the leadership of Wells, were there to meet them when they arrived. Even a company of high school cadets, an organization formed after the Spanish-American War in most high schools, was called into action and armed with old Civil War Springfield rifles and bayonets, although no ammunition was issued.

The National Guard surrounded the railroad depot. Others formed a square in the street in front of the depot. A Gattling gun was set up a hundred yards north of the depot; the Citizens Alliance, carrying pistols, lined the street a block north of them. When the train arrived, ten to fifteen shots were fired from the gun toward the mountainside over the depot roof. As the deportees left the train they were marched into the square and then to Redman's where they were held until preparations were ready for their departure by special train.

The arrival of martial law ended the crisis, but whether such a drastic measure was necessary was hotly argued. In the East, especially in Ohio and New York, public outcry about the lawlessness in Colorado and the deplorable, uncivilized state of affairs in Telluride created banner headlines.

Bad as times were, they might have been worse. It

was later learned that the radical element within the Miners' Union, especially Harry Orchard, had seriously considered getting even with Telluride by rolling bombs full of dynamite down the hill into town or poisoning the municipal reservoir with cyanide. That he was capable of such activity is corroborated by the fact that he later blew up the depot at Cripple Creek, killing thirteen men and injuring twenty-six others, and that he killed a former governor of Idaho by wiring a bomb to his gate.

Subsequent years also led to a partial solution of the mystery surrounding the death of Arthur Collins. Adams, Bulkeley Wells' would-be assassin, offered to show the sheriff in Telluride the scenes of various unexplained crimes if he were allowed to "fork a horse." Officials agreed to his wish, and Adams proceeded to show them where the shotgun which killed Collins had been thrown after the murder. He also offered to show them the remains of Barney, the Smuggler-Union shift boss who mysteriously disappeared during the strike. It turned out that Barney had been shot near the livery stable and thrown into the bushes one night by union men. When the odor became strong, they moved the body into the heavy timber along the Alta Mine road. The bones had been scattered by coyotes, but a skull covered with red hair was found indicating that Adams was telling the truth. The remains were exhibited in a Telluride store window to convince union sympathizers that murder had been committed.

About the only thing unaffected by the years of labor-management disputes was the mail, which would have brought in federal investigators. Fortunately this fact helped keep a few men alive on one occasion and saved a life another time. During the 1903 strike a strike-breaker leader was holed up in a mine with his men, surrounded by hostile miners. The union men were trying to starve out the scabs; nothing could enter or leave the mine except the U.S. mail. The scab leader managed to order food by mail, which arrived on pack-horses, properly stamped. The strikers knew what was happening and debated bitterly whether to let it through. Fear of tampering with the federal mail eventually determined the course of the argument, and the scabs ate ravenously.

The same leader, having established a technique to relieve the siege, stuffed one of his injured men, who badly needed medical attention, into a mail sack. The mail carrier weighed, stamped, and addressed the man to the hospital. He went past the strikers on a pack mule and received medical care that saved his life.

It was interesting to learn how sharp-witted some men had been during trying times (and there was an element of curiosity satisfied in solving some of the previously unanswered questions), but the predominant feeling was that the time was one best forgotten. Whether right or wrong, martial law had ended the crisis. The tragic chapter was one to leave to the past.

Gunfights, murder, natural disaster. It was part of a tragic scenario which, had it been staged, would have been critized as unrealistically exaggerated. The only proper criticism, however, would have been that the script was understated. In the years between the labor problems and the arrival of the First World War, the town would also watch helplessly as disaster took to the water and also rode the rails of the Southern.

In a short article that typified the ebullient optimism of the early '90s, the *Journal* of February 21, 1891, noted:

The stage to Rico from Telluride had a narrow escape from wreckage by a snowslide before reaching Trout Lake; a slide in its rushing, downward progress carried down the whole outfit. Fortunately, no damage was done, neither horses, sleigh, nor driver being seriously hurt. This will be avoided when the Denver and Rio Grande Southern is located far away from any danger of that kind.

Time proved the error in judgment as the Southern became involved in accidents the likes of which passengers on the old stage never could have imagined. Billy Whistler, the engineer of a ten-wheeler, was killed when his engine overturned near Glencoe. A little later Jimmy Stewart met the same fate a few miles west of Durango. In 1906 the whole end of a train, including five cars and the caboose, went through the trestle twelve miles north of Rico, killing the conductor and maiming members of the crew. Two years earlier an engine went through a bridge south of Dolores, killing the fireman. In 1918 Engineer Peake was killed when his engine hit a weakened span and crashed.

In 1909 an incident occurred which momentarily thrust Telluride back thirty years in time. A great accumulation of water proved too much for the dam at Trout Lake. The onrushing water gave rise to the tale

Courtesy of Homer Reid Collection

Derailed freight cars on the Rio Grande Southern

As if labor problems weren't
enough, disaster also rode the
rails with alarming frequency.

about the calculating Pinheads, but it took out nearly
sixteen miles of railroad as well. Telluride became an
isolated town whose supplies were brought in by
mules and wagons as they had been for the pioneers in
the '80s. And like their rugged predecessors, their
wants remained simple and unaffected. The first train
to reach town was loaded with the only really essential
item: kegs and kegs of beer.

The year 1914 brought the discovery of uranium
and vanadium, and with it an inrush of new capital. In
retrospect the year became not one of new hopes but of
the terrible flood. Barely five years after the breaking
of the dam, Telluride would again witness the destruc-
tive power of a great quantity of uncontrolled water.

Cornet Creek, which flows down the mountain on the north side of the valley, is normally a charming gush of water that provided the name for the local turn-of-the-century band. When a cloudburst struck high on the side of the mountain it was beyond the capacity of the creek to carry the accumulating runoff quietly in its bed. A full-scale flood was in the making, and even had the people known about it there was little that could have been done. The rushing stream picked up a mill dump containing waste rock that had been crushed to dust by the mill. The water dissolved it into a syrupy conglomerate spiced with boulders and then swept through the town. A woman drowned, homes were turned on end or crushed, and the lobby of the Sheridan Hotel filled with mud almost to the ceiling. Anyone who had to walk down the street was confronted with chest-high ooze.

Courtesy of San Miguel County Museum

The beer train was the first to arrive after water temporarily washed out the railroad in 1909.

Oak Street after Cornet Creek went over its banks in 1914

Another view of damage on Oak Street from the 1914 flood

Mud, slime, and high-water marks in the Sheridan bar, 1914 flood

In order to clean up, local carpenters built a long flume through the middle of town, something like the sluice boxes in mining. People took fire hoses and washed the mud, wood, and rocks into the flume and on to the river. In time the debris was picked up and the buildings were cleaned out, but high-water marks, mud, and slime were in corners and on walls for a long time.

As if problems with nature were not sufficient, the Colorado Legislature decided in 1915 that the public health, safety, and welfare would be better served if alcohol no longer existed in the state. On December 31, 1915, more than three years before the national prohibition amendment became effective, Colorado and of course Telluride, went legally dry.

The years of World War I came along, and Telluride joined the rest of the country in raising a patriotic cry to defeat the enemy overseas. The pages of the *Journal*

World War I headline in the *Journal*

were filled with praise for those who were aiding the cause and scorn for those shameless few who were not. Economically, however, the town was beginning to suffer. The cost of mining was increasing, but the value of ore was remaining fairly steady. By the '20s most of the mines had shut down.

Poor Telluride couldn't even buy a new fire truck without experiencing tragedy. For years fire fighting had been the duty of Lee Long and his two well-trained horses, Beachy and Barny, who pulled the wagons on solid steel tires to the fires in town. On June 24, 1920, a fire broke out at the Smuggler-Union mill. Long was making the evening rounds with the night marshall and was halfway back to the station when the fire bell rang. Although it wasn't customary, several firemen harnessed Beachy and Barny, and when Long arrived they gave him the reins. Long felt something was wrong. He shouted out to close the station doors, but no one heard. Long's intuition was justified; one of the check reins was loose.

The well-trained horses, knowing their master had the reins, charged out of the station as they always had, and the wagon raced wildly out of control down Fir Street. One of the firemen fell off the wagon in front of the express office, another jumped off near the Telluride Garage. Others either jumped or fell free, leaving Lee alone on the truck.

He ignored urgings to jump, striving desperately to regain control of his frightened team. The horses reached the railroad siding and bolted through an opening between two freight cars that were protruding halfway across the street. The animals made it though the opening, but a wheel of the wagon caught the corner of a freight car, and Lee Long was thrown forward underneath the wheels. His skull was crushed upon impact. Art Elkamp, who had followed the wagon in his truck, reached the scene seconds after Lee was

Courtesy of San Miguel County Museum

Beachy and Barney in happier moments

thrown off, but there was nothing he could do. Two firemen helped place Lee in the truck and they rushed to the hospital, where Lee Long was pronounced dead on arrival.

The accident left the team uninjured but slowed them enough that Roy Hogan was finally able to grab the reins. All available cars were rushed to the mill, but it took more than an hour before the equipment arrived. During that time the Smuggler-Union mill burned to the ground at a loss estimated between $125,000 and $250,000. Acting as head of the Smuggler-Union properties, Bulkeley Wells, on the very day of the fire, offered $2,000 toward obtaining a motorized fire truck. The tragedy made everyone realize the necessity, and city officials managed to raise $5,000 to buy a new truck.

It was a nostalgic morning when a shiny, new truck drove up and forever replaced the old but polished No.

Courtesy of San Miguel County Museum

A shiny truck but a sad day: the horse-drawn fire wagon was a thing of the past

1 red wagon that had always charged down the street behind Beachy and Barny with Lee Long at the reins. The old horses perked up their ears and raced across the pasture toward the fire station whenever the bell was rung in the years that followed, but the day of the horse-drawn fire wagon had come to an end.

In the light of two decades of such events, it is surprising to find a picture of a passenger car on the Southern bearing a banner proclaiming, "TELLURIDE — THE TOWN WITHOUT A BELLY-ACHE." The occasion was a baseball game in Durango in the early '20s. Many of the supporters on their way to the game decided they needed a slogan.

Why such a slogan? What went on to make life so bearable during those trying twenty years? The answer lies in part in the character of the men and women who made up the town. Whatever other businesses were

Courtesy of Homer Reid Collection

The Mule Skinners' Ball was an annual highlight not to be missed for the likes of train wrecks, floods, or anything else.

there, Telluride was still primarily a mining town, and the people had the eternal optimism of the prospector. They also lived with the conviction that life was hard. Good times were to be enjoyed; bad times were to be expected. All would work out in the long run.

In terms of cold economics, the mines had produced over $60 million worth of precious metals by 1909. Of equal importance in the eyes of many, by the end of the first decade the Mule Skinner's Ball at Redmond's was a firmly established attraction and by itself was enough to overcome a man's woes. The invitations were printed on white pack canvas in old English letters:

Yourself and ladies are invited to attend the Mule Skinner's Ball at the Opera House, Telluride, Colorado, March tenth, nineteen hundred eleven.

Come hired gunmen or high water, strikes or martial law, the ball was an annual highlight that was well attended.

By 1914 there was a new opera house up from the Sheridan, and all kinds of traveling stock companies and entertainers came to perform. The local Rocky Mountain Players put on *H.M.S. Pinafore,* and there was always a dance going on where you could do the Glide, Black Eagle, Highland Fling, Sailor's Hornpipe, Virginia Reel, or Russian Steppe Dance. Just keeping up with the dashing Bulkeley Wells was enough to occupy a quiet evening.

Wells was frequently seen around town in his elegant horse-drawn carriage and was well known for his lavish parties and immaculate dress. Over the years he had acquired a reputation for being a man who had time for everyone. He was never known to cut a con-

Courtesy of San Miguel County Museum

Mule Skinners' Ball advertisement on white pack canvas

versation short. He was friendly to his acquaintances and courteous to strangers. More than one good friend was known to have received a short-term lease on a good vein in the Smuggler that would bring up to $50,000 for doing practically nothing. But the real intrigue concerned what Bulkeley was doing in Denver.

Wells' unquestionable flair and exciting personality resulted in his being at the focal point of Denver society. His parties were known to be lively because of his presence and lavish because of his devoted admirer, Mrs. Crawford Hill — many years his senior and leading Denver socialite. In 1918 Bulkeley's wife, the former Grace Livermore, divorced him on grounds of deserting her and their four children. Crawford Hill died in 1922, but Wells never married Mrs. Hill, much to her chagrin. By the time her friends, the Whitneys, severed Wells from their mining ventures, he had spent between $8 and $11 million of the Whitney fortune. During his final year he reportedly spent $75,000 of Whitney money for personal expenses alone.

Wells did marry the beautiful daughter of a local Telluride boardinghouse keeper. The humiliation was too much for his former Denver friend, and Wells was quietly offered $12,000 a year to disappear. Out of personal pride he refused the offer, but eventually he had to leave in search of work. He moved to Nevada where he worked as a consulting engineer. He later moved to San Francisco. Unsuccessful oil ventures and gambling reduced his financial resources, and at age 65 he found himself a broken, forgotten man. Unwilling to sell the thousands of dollars worth of knick-knacks he had accumulated in happier days, Bulkeley Wells borrowed $20, bought a gun, and shot himself.

By the time Wells had reached the tragic end of his life, he had been long departed from Telluride. He would have recalled with ease, however, that momentous day in the pre-World War I era when some adven-

turous soul drove a car into town for the first time. It
was a Carter. It had to be pulled over Keystone Hill on
a dry day to get there, but it arrived.

Shortly after, in 1915, the Methodist Church was
bought and converted into a recreation building. Those
who wanted to play basketball had a hardwood floor to
play on. A baseball diamond was established at the east
end of town, and it wasn't long before a quarter-mile
straightaway was put in by the train depot for horse racing. Another racetrack was located out of town, just east
of "Society Turn" (today's road to Rico), where society
people would take their carriages for a Sunday ride,
turn around, and drive back to town. On the Fourth of
July the Navajos would come in from New Mexico with
their fast ponies, bet on the races, and demonstrate
their beautiful blankets.

There was no lack of colorful characters. Over the
years came Christmas Tree John, Old Dick Liner the
Moonshiner, Toss-em-Up, Monkey Wrench, and old
Step and a Half. In place of the eccentric Lon Remine,
there was McMann, who divorced his wife and divided
their house on Galena Street with boards. Half the
house was his, half was hers, but he preferred to stay
wherever he found himself at the end of the day. Like
Remine, McMann ate out of one filthy bowl, day in and
day out.

If the winters were hard and Telluride became difficult to reach, corn and wheat intended for animals
would be ground up in coffee mills and used for bread.
If the local newspaper ran out of newsprint, it could
commandeer all the paper in town — including the
butcher's wrapping paper. He could sell his meat on
sharp sticks.

Even the Southern could provide a laugh when it
wasn't running off the tracks or losing its brakes. On
one occasion, Bosco the Snake Charmer left his snakes
at Vance Junction after giving a show in Telluride.

Conductor Sanders told him he couldn't take his snakes on the passenger train to Rico but they would be put on the next freight train. Colonel Vance, who usually got drunk on payday, was experiencing a monthly round of the DT's. He was chasing big green grasshoppers on the hillside when acting agent John Houk told him he had a suitcase full of live snakes in the office. The colonel entered the office, announced he wasn't afraid of any kind of snake, grabbed an armful out of the suitcase, and scattered them on the floor. There were dozens of rattlers and watersnakes, among others. Houk spent the day sweeping snakes out of the office, Vance fell into a state of semishock when he realized what he had done, and Bosco cursed the railroad all the way to Rico when he learned that half his act had last been seen wriggling into the bushes.

Another sure way to cope with the hard times was to ignore the cause. This wasn't always possible, but, in the case of a legislature that didn't appreciate the value of an occasional good drink, it was more than possible; it was necessary.

After Colorado went dry on the last day of 1915, alcohol was shipped in, until Congress passed the Volstead Act in 1919 which resulted in the prohibition amendment to the Constitution. Then began the days of bootleg liquor from Canada and Mexico. It didn't take long for a few people in Telluride to realize that spirits could be obtained with more safety and at less cost if they went into business for themselves. Maybe the mines weren't producing and there wasn't much industry around, but, with a practicality and shrewdness their grandfathers would have been proud of, several residents began experimenting in the art of moonshining.

It was logical that anyone used to dealing in first-class ore wouldn't put out a second-class product. Some eventually came to say that Telluride whiskey "made

with pure mountain water" was in demand in New
York. There were days when nine tons of sugar would
come into town without an ounce going to the stores.
On one occasion Don O'Rourke was returning with a
truckload when a policeman asked what he was doing
with all that sugar. "I'm going back to Telluride," he
replied. "We're making sugar candy there, you know."

The stills eventually replaced the madams of old as
providers for the city treasury. A $500 "soft drink" tax
was imposed on the more than fifty refreshment parlors
in town. No city levy was imposed on local citizens.
Everyone participated one way or another, and anyone
who could turn out something good enough to bring
funds into town was a public benefactor.

It was hardly a small-time operation. Besides the
numerous "local suppliers," there were ten wholesale
manufacturers who exported their production. One
man didn't even bother with a still. He boiled his mash
in a big tub, put an old horse blanket on top of the tub,
and waited until the blanket was saturated with steam.

Courtesy of Irene Wichmann

A sign of industry and a public benefactor

Photograph by Suzanne C. Fetter

The Telluride Brewery today. The buildings stand to the east of town on the north side of the road.

Then it was just a question of wringing out the moonshine. Consumers agreed that the smoke and ash, not to mention the horsehair, enhanced the flavor beyond belief.

You could get a drink anywhere: the courthouse, the office of the Civil Works Administration, homes, and soda parlors. In Peterson's Garage, which was where the Hole-in-the-Wall Pizza place now stands, there was a liqour-making operation in the basement. At times the revenue man would come through to check things out. He would drop in at Peterson's, where there was an ice-cream parlor. The owner would tip off his cohorts in the basement with a secret signal, and a Gay Nineties soda jerk would keep the officer busy with a free ice-cream soda. By the time he got around to checking out the basement there would be nothing to see but a friendly card game going an and a few cups of coffee or soda pop being consumed. The illegal barrels had been loaded on a wooden slide in a specially constructed chute and shoved into the next building for safekeeping.

They used a different technique at the Ress House, on East Columbia Avenue and North Alder. Here there were wine shelves stocked with fruit. When the shelves were opened you could help yourself to a bottle of wine.

On one occasion the law got out the bloodhounds and came from Montrose to look for someone who had robbed a grocery store and was reportedly hiding out around Telluride. The dogs had been trained to sniff out stills as well; they caused a few unexpected revelations. Basically the law left Telluride alone. Isolation did a lot to keep investigators from bothering to check what was going on, and the lay of the valley served to thwart those who did. The prohibition enforcement agent, Jack McFall, had only to set out from Montrose and within minutes there was a call of warning to Telluride. John Snodgrass of Placerville had a good view up the canyon, and he would keep a lookout for McFall's arrival. One day Dr. Parker, the Telluride town doctor, was out of town on a medical visit when he saw a car speeding up the canyon. Two young men were aboard — one at the wheel, the other on the running board hanging on to a boiler with coils attached. Moments later along came agent McFall. When he arrived in Telluride the soda fountains and fruit shelves were waiting for him.

After all, the towns was producing good stuff. No one ever went blind, became paralized, died, or got hurt — unless he drank "Jamaica Ginger," but that was a foreign import and didn't count.

Unfortunately, resourcefulness, pluck, and optimism weren't enough. Telluride was caught up in something bigger than itself. The entire country, as the '20s passed, headed toward the Great Depression. Like a nasty fly refusing to let a game but tired horse alone, fate continued to harrass the town. In 1926 several local men made an attempt to reopen and rework the Black Bear Mine. A small crew went there, moved into the old boardinghouse, and went to work. On March 21, some of them went to town for a break, leaving five men behind. On March 22 a blizzard struck. On April 2 an avalanche roared down the mountain, but it didn't touch the boardinghouse where the five were staying. That night, while all the residents were asleep, a second avalanche split the house in half, shredding it to pieces down the slope. A few people were buried but unhurt, and they came out alive. One man and one woman were killed. The attempt to maintain the operation of the Black Bear continued through other such incidents. Storms and slides over the years finally closed the mine in 1934.

Two more lives were lost in the Ajax slide of 1928. In the same year the suffering economy brought about the end of the Tomboy, truly one of the old reliables that had been producing since "Tomboy" Thomas discovered it in 1886.

The Bank of Telluride closed in September 1929, and as the depression years wore on the population tumbled to a mere 512. Telluride lost its priest and again became a mission of Montrose sixty-five miles away. There were no paved roads, and no regular mass was held. The solitude of the 1880s fell upon the town without the tough men of the cloth who once braved Ophir Pass every Sunday to clear the bar and hold a meeting. The Pick & Gad, Idle Hour, Big Swede, and the cribs were still open, but the main street was a far cry from the exuberant days of the bullwhackers, mule trains, and celebrating miners on a binge. But Telluride didn't die — and never considered the thought. Legal or not, that supply of sugar became the economic lifeblood of the town.

The realization that a depression was going to hit came to some men before others. One who knew was

Charles Delos Waggoner, president of the Bank of Telluride. "Buck," as he was called, knew what it would mean. Most of his clients were his friends. They were hardworking miners, cattlemen, and laborers. When the day came that his bank couldn't pay its creditors, their life savings would be gone.

No one knows how long it took for Waggoner to devise his plan, for he confided in not a single person in or out of town. The night before he left Telluride he stayed up playing cards with one of his good friends until around one in the morning, as he often did, and by daybreak he was gone.

Waggoner went to Denver and sent six telegrams to New York City, each to a large prosperous bank. Using the code of the American Bankers' Association, he instructed each bank to deposit an amount of $75,000 or $100,000 with The Chase National Bank in Denver for transfer to the Bank of Telluride. The message was signed by six of the leading banks in Denver. Seeing nothing unusual in the request, the New York banks complied as a routine matter.

On August 31, the small, well-dressed banker nervously presented his credentials to the Central Hanover Bank in New York and paid off a Bank of Telluride note for $250,000 and a personal note for $60,000. He then ordered a check for $180,000. The transactions were verified by the Chase National Bank and drawn against the Bank of Telluride's $500,000 credit now deposited with Chase. After repaying his bank's debts, Waggoner disappeared from New York.

When banking officials became aware of the swindle, there was an uproar. Cables and telegrams flew between Denver and New York as the banks tried desperately and unsuccessfully to recover the money and place blame for the loss. Waggoner had signed six names to his original telegrams, hoping that those Denver banks would have to bear the loss. Years be-

Courtesy of Homer Reid Collection

The Pennsylvania in 1927, like the mines in the late '20s, was falling to its knees

fore, he had lent them gold when they were shaky, but when his own hard times came they refused to lend him a hand. He felt it fair that they bear the loss. However, they had only performed the legitimate business of issuing money against drafts sent by the New York banks and thus emerged unscathed by his scheme.

Rumors had the "seedy country banker," as the *New York Times* called him, in Mexico, Canada, and even in a Graf Zeppelin bound for Europe. He was finally found in New Castle, Wyoming, and arrested by federal agents. Waggoner seemed relieved to be caught and surrendered quietly. Only $400 was found on him, and he said that he only wanted to protect his creditors. "I would rather see the New York banks lose money than the people of Telluride, most of whom have worked all their lives for the savings that were deposited in my bank," Waggoner said to the federal men.

The quiet, bespectacled little man waived his hearing in Cheyenne and agreed to a trial in New York. He was shackled hand and foot and transported to New York by a U.S. marshall and two special guards. The trial was held October 10, and Waggoner pleaded guilty. Asked if he wanted to say anything before sentencing, he said, "I'd like to tell you something about Telluride," and he went on to describe the breakup of the mining industry and the decline of cattle raising. He described the subsequent hard times and poverty in his town. "I'm not sorry. I had to do it," he said. "The New York banks merely loaned me $500,000 for the use of the Bank of Telluride. They would have received their money back. It would have been a good loan for them, but I couldn't convince them of that until after I had the money."

His lawyer tried to present him as a Robin Hood trying to help his people, but Judge Frank J. Colman sentenced him to fifteen years. Judge Colman wrote to the parole board, however, urging parole after a three-year term. "Buck" Waggoner, aged 56, emerged from prison. Gone were the friends, respect, and security he had spent a lifetime building. He was a controversial figure back home. Some had seen their savings safeguarded; others had not. Some pointed out his using funds for his own affairs as well.

All the man had left were a few newspaper clippings and a prison record. He had a hard time finding a job. He tried unsuccessfully to start a bakery in Georgia and was later arrested but not prosecuted on gambling charges. Waggoner wound up in Grand Junction, Colorado, where J. Walter Eames, an old Telluride acquaintance, gladly gave a job to the old friend who had once given him a $500 loan when he had been desperate. Then Eames was shot and killed in a holdup at his Baltimore Club, and Waggoner drifted on to Reno. Within a few years he went blind and then died.

Preston Walker, editor of the *Grand Junction Sentinel*, called Waggoner "the only guy from Colorado, or perhaps anywhere, I guess, who took those New York guys." Despite his efforts, the bank folded. The last check was issued in 1934 in a building just down the street from where Butch Cassidy and his Hole-in-the-Wall gang had started lives of crime forty-five years before. The bank would not reopen for the next thirty years.

When Dr. Parker arrived in the mid-'30s to take the place of Telluride's only doctor, prosperity was far from being just around the corner. Time and the Roosevelt administration had set in motion steps that would bring the country out of the depression, but in Telluride there were still people who paid their doctor bill with rabbits, valued at three per dollar. Health standards were low, and Mrs. East, state inspector for the Department of Health, threatened regularly to close down the hospital. Each time she threatened, the doctor agreed it would be a good idea.

The hospital used a form of anesthesia known as the "drip-mask" method, which used ether dripped onto a piece of folded gauze held over the patient's nose. It was safer than chloroform but not without risk, especially when the power failed. The danger of explosion was too great to use a kerosene lamp, so Dr. Parker rapidly became skilled at performing surgery, delivering babies, and setting fractures in the dark. One exception was when Charley Ross was practically scalped when his car went off Norwood Hill. The lights went out while Dr. Parker was cleaning the wound of gravel, glass, and debris, and the job was finished by using a flashlight.

Toward the end of the '30s the mines began to reopen, and Dr. Parker was hired by the Argentine Mine at $400 a month to make a weekly trip to Rico to look after the two hundred people who comprised the employees of the mine and their families. In the event of a serious mine accident the doctor injected a shot of morphine and strapped the injured man into a cage so he could be brought to the surface. This old mining rescue technique of "basket cases" gave rise to the expression and was a device that saw frequent use. Being a mining doctor required a head for climbing as well as a knowledge of medicine. On many occasions the doctor had to reach his patient by ladder, climbing as far as 400 feet up or down to render aid.

The unusual was the rule rather than the exception, and it took something extraordinary to raise an eyebrow over a medical event in Telluride — but George C. Balderston did just that in 1940. Then a practicing physician at the hospital, Balderston performed an appendectomy on himself at the local hospital with another doctor in attendance. The task was completed in forty-five minutes, and two days later he was back at work.

It was early one morning in 1940 that Dr. Parker stopped at the Roma Cafe and saw Phil Novak setting up drinks for everyone. Parker was surprised because he knew that Novak had been broke for a month. Later in the day he met Jack Patrick, Novak's partner in a leased-mined venture. Patrick was obviously unhappy. "Somebody stole our high grade," he said. The next day Novak's body was found in an alley with seventeen knife wounds. The heart had been punctured seven times, the windpipe severed three times. The coroner in Norwood declared a suicide, which was the best way to clear up an unpleasant matter with a minimum of complications.

What had happened was clear, and the coroner had

ruled according to the code of the mountains. Novak and Patrick had agreed to share the proceeds of the mining venture on a basis of percentage of tonnage and value. Novak had robbed his partner blind. A few weeks later Patrick paid a visit to Dr. Parker's office. "Jack, you sure got out of that knifing slick and clean," the doctor said. Patrick made no comment and no denials. He figured he had it coming and that was the end of it. The old code that had governed conduct in the '80s and '90s had not died out.

The extent to which high-grading was carried on in 1940 was, however, quite a shocking matter. High-grading was simply another word for stealing. A miner might find an extra rich vein and take six or seven pounds of ore, about $100 worth, out of the mine with him when he went home for the day. A little under his coat or in his lunch pail went by unnoticed as he left. Wages had improved considerably since the days of the labor disputes, but if the Lord wanted to place an extra rich vein in front of a man, sort of as compensation for inadequate wages, a few ounces here and there surely wouldn't be missed by the management. If a man got caught, the usual excuse for having the ore would be a small mining claim up in the hills. One man testified in court that he had brought the ore out of a mine at Ophir. He received a year in the federal penitentiary when it was pointed out that Ophir was under twenty feet of snow at the alleged time.

Twelve local men organized a serious high-grading operation that year and set up a local saloon as the center of activity. A concentration mill was set up in the basement so the ore could be prepared for sale on the market. It was difficult for the mining company to crack the operation because so many people were involved in one way or another. Smelters, dental-supply houses, jewelers, buyers of new and old gold were all part of a potential market. Even banks would buy gold dust with no questions asked.

Miners would get $5 for $35 worth of ore. Occasionally the scales would be tipped so the miners got less, but two high-graders once got the better of a fence. They took a steel ball the size of a baseball and gold-plated it with a shell of gold an inch thick. The fence paid $15 an ounce. The miners took their payment and cleared out, leaving the fence several hundred dollars short when the fraud was exposed.

When the local high-grading operation was finally uncovered, the town buzzed the most in a long time. The paper said that not since banker Waggoner's escapade in 1929 had Telluride seen such excitement. The entire high-grading incident involved between $50,000 and $100,000 of ore stolen from the Smuggler-Union and the Tomboy. All twelve conspirators were eventually arrested. The miner who lived near the hospital returned the baby scales he had borrowed "to weigh vegetables raised in his garden to sell to his neighbors." After the bits of gold dust and quartz were removed, the scales were put back into use.

Individual resources could be feathered now and then by an illicit operation, innovative doctors could keep the town healthy and on its feet; but even the most drastic surgery and the most unusual innovation in railroading could not lead to the ultimate preservation of the old Southern.

In the forty years following the financial problems which struck the Colorado and Rio Grande Southern in 1895, tonnage declined steadily, and deficits surpassed $2 million. In 1930 the line again passed into receivership. The receiver, Victor A. Miller, turned down the nomination for state attorney general in order to try to save the Southern. His chief mechanic, Jack Oden-

Hard times, high-grading, and World War II failed to daunt some, like this prospector photographed on the Fourth of July 1941.

paugh, tried desperately to make railroading profitable by designing a rail bus that became known as "The Galloping Goose." The Galloping Goose was nothing more than a truck on rails. There was room for freight and about seven passengers. Power came from either a Buick, Winton, or Pierce-Arrow motor.

The name for the strange vehicle originated either when one of the engineers told two school teacher tourists they "had better hurry and get aboard if they wanted to ride this galloping goose to Ridway," or when a lady who disliked the contraption that had replaced regular passenger trains disdainfully remarked about "that galloping goose coming down the track." Whatever the origin, the name stuck, and the railroad had a galloping goose designed and painted on the side of the vehicle.

The first Galloping Goose went into use on June 1, 1931, powered by a Buick engine. The last one was put into service in October 1936. In 1933 the price of gold

rose to $35 an ounce, and there was a temporary revival
of activity around Telluride. The Goose served the
mines as its less peculiar predecessors had in earlier
years. By the late 1940s the Goose had become a popular tourist attraction, the trip over the big Ophir loop
stunning people with its height and magnificent scenery as it had in the days of Otto Mears. Excursion tick-
ets to Durango could be bought for $3, and the run
from Dolores to Ridgway could be made in eight hours
and fifty-three minutes.

Some trips took much longer.

One January day found three passengers and the
driver trapped by drifts at the top of 10,200-foot Lizard
Head Pass. The Goose had been following a steam engine which was clearing the track. The locomotive
halted, unable to move. Howling winds arose and
closed in. A second locomotive steamed out of Rico
with a rescue crew of four and also got stuck. Rescuers
set out again, this time on snowshoes. This time they
reached the stranded passengers. The Goose had an oil
stove, but food was low. One man tapped a telephone
circuit and called for help. Two pilots took off in planes
from Cortez and flew into the storm to drop food and
fuel. When the weather cleared a week later, rescue
locomotives managed to push their way through and all
were saved.

Three times within two months the Goose thrilled
its passengers by having brake trouble. The first time
there was a lady aboard with two children, aged four
and seven. The woman grabbed the four-year-old girl
and leaped into a soft snowbank. The Goose gained
speed, and the driver grabbed the seven-year-old boy
and jumped safely into another snowbank. A few weeks
later the same thing happened; this time the driver and
four passengers jumped to safety. The Goose rolled
precariously for eleven miles around curves and over

"The Galloping Goose," unparalleled in railroad history, was the last gasp of a dying railroad.

trestles, stopping finally and safely — a little ahead of schedule — in front of Ridgway Station.

On the third occasion the driver, who was alone, jumped clear of the runaway Goose. The Goose raced down the canyon, made two tight turns, left the tracks, and plummeted into a gorge. The battered car was brought up and put back into service. But what descendant of the old Southern could not be excused for leaving the tracks at least once?

During World War II, Prof. Albert Einstein told President Roosevelt that uranium oxide, a byproduct of vanadium that had been tossed away and ignored for years, had a certain value. Suddenly the lines of the old Southern were filled with a highly valuable deposit guarded by federal agents with machine guns. In a supreme final irony, the train that was stuffing its valve

Courtesy of Homer Reid Collection

The Rio Grande Southern served Telluride and the San Juans through the twentieth century without much financial assistance.

Courtesy of Homer Reid Collection

After World War II the railroad rapidly declined

Courtesy of Homer Reid Collection

A shiny engine of the RGS

Courtesy of Homer Reid Collection

Faithful servant in all kinds of weather

with old shirts and going along the rails in its final
years was carrying a cargo important enough to help
end a world war, alter the world, and obliterate two
faraway cities in Japan named Nagasaki and Hiroshima.

Soon after the war ended, the Southern lost its mail
contract and tourist travel declined. Dissatisfaction
with the service, due in large part to poor management,
had been growing since the early '40s. More than once
the managers of the Telluride mines heatedly
threatened to remove their business from the railroad.
Finally, in December 1949, the operation was abandoned and the entire system was placed on sale. On
September 30, 1951, with a debt of $9 million (nearly
the same amount Otto Mears had raised to build the
line in 1890) the railroad came to an end.

The last steam passenger train ran from Ridgway,
via Telluride, to Lizard Head, and back. This was an

Courtesy of Homer Reid Collection

Battling a snowbank

Courtesy of Homer Reid Collection

The last trip of the Southern,
1951.

excursion sponsored by the Rocky Mountain Railroad
Club in 1951, and 129 passengers from Colorado, surrounding states, the Midwest, and as far away as New
York, New Jersey, and California came to pay their
final respects to a grand old railroad and to witness the
end of an era in American railroading.

Many people hoped that, if the railroad had to go, at
least the records could be perserved. A federal judge
assigned them to the Colorado State Historical Society,
but the records never arrived in Denver. Officials, employees, bribers, and looters managed to "acquire" the
records at Ridgway, where they were supposed to be
under guard. A few remnants were bought by the Narrow Gauge Motel at Alamosa and later transferred to
the Colorado Railroad Museum at Golden. The records
at Durango fell into the hands of someone with access
to the office and were never seen again.

Galloping Goose service ended October 26, 1951, the last train running from Telluride to Ridgway. During the following year, bits and pieces of the line fell into public and private hands throughout Colorado and outside the state. Galloping Goose No. 4, purchased with donations from organizations and individuals interested in preserving it, became the property of the Telluride Fire Department in 1952. It rests next to the county courthouse today, the descendant of Otto Mears, creation of Jack Odenpaugh, servant of President Roosevelt, and curiosity of the present.

With the Southern gone, Telluride declined to a city with five bars, one weekly newspaper, one hotel, one tourist court, a few ministers, one doctor, one lawyer, one dentist, and no bank. The town was weak and ready for a death blow which struck on April 27, 1953.

Telluride Mines, Inc., which had purchased the Tomboy and adjoining mines in 1942, announced it would shut down due to losses. The mines had provided the lifeblood of the town. Now this vital last artery was severed. Ironically, statistics showed that San Miguel County lead Colorado in retail production that year.

The *Rocky Mountain News* carried the story on the following day under a headline announcing, "Historic Telluride Mines to Shut Down." Two hundred and thirty workers, representing 90 percent of the male work force in town, faced unemployment. Over the preceding two years the mine had invested $1.5 million dollars in improvements, but with lead at 12 cents per pound and zinc at 11 cents, profit was impossible. Operations had been at a loss for two years and couldn't continue any longer. Even the vice-president and general manager of the mine, Charles F. Parker, Jr., couldn't believe what had happened. "The entire economy of the town was built around the mines. There's nothing left." he said.

The old railroad station, still part of the "time capsule" that is Telluride

Reaction among the townspeople was summed up by Mrs. Iris C. Lein, editor and publisher of the *Telluride Tribune*:

There was a lack of foresight among us in not making Telluride a great tourist attraction to buffet such an economic blow. I suggest most of the families here — most of the workers are permanent residents, not floaters — will move away. It's like the death of a loved one.

Not all the voices were cries of despair, however. It is interesting to note that Telluride's true colors were struck by a 60-year-old man who had lived all his life in the town. In 1953, August R. Gustafson, then the mayor, spoke from a keen knowledge of the nature of his hometown:

I've lived here all my life and seen all the ups and downs of the mining industry. I remember when gold was the big thing — and lead and zinc just by products. And I've seen that situation reversed.

I remember when the mines closed during other depressions. But they always came back.

We have the minerals here in our mines — and we'll have them for a long time. All we need is a right price for them — and we'll get them yet.

I suppose it'll be tough sledding for a lot of the folks here. Some of them will probably move away. But Telluride will come back.

Unknown to August Gustafson, Mrs. Lein, and probably even to Manager Parker, steps that would lead to the saving of Telluride had already been initiated. Almost as if Fortune had decided to amuse herself by smiling again on the small town she had for so long ignored, Telluride's luck finally changed for the better just when all seemed lost.

On May 12, barely two weeks after the announcement of the closing of Telluride Mines, Inc., banner headlines proclaimed, "TELLURIDE SAVED!" The Idarado Mining Company was going to buy out the old Telluride Mines, Inc.

Idarado, a subsidiary of Newmont Mining Company of New York, began as a consolidation of several old mines in the late '30s, including the Black Bear, Treasury Tunnel, Barstow, and Imogene. By 1953 it had acquired practically every mine in the mountain at Telluride. The Smuggler, Liberty Bell, Tomboy, Montana, Ajax, Argentine, and countless other veins were all under Idarado's domain. The entire operation was connected by a system of tunnels that wended in and out of the mountain. The system was extensive enough to allow a man, if he knew where he was going, to enter the mine on the Telluride side of the mountain and exit above Ouray on the opposite side.

In 1955 production was halted temporarily to construct a million dollar mill which would process 1,800 tons of ore per day. By 1964 miners were producing as much ore, and the modern mill at Pandora was turning out as much concentrate, as was produced by all the mines in the region during the boom at the turn of the century.

Telluride, thanks to the arrival of Idarado at the eleventh hour, turned a significant corner. It would not, like South Pass City in Wyoming, Virginia City in Montana, and countless other towns in Colorado and throughout the West, become a ghost town whose faded shingles, broken windows, and sagging rooftops would provide a crumbling reminder of the American past. Rather it would be a living reminder of a very lively, if bygone, day. Traveling through Telluride in 1961, J. R. Humphreys referred to the town as a place for the "purist time traveler." He wrote:

> The women are no longer at the windows, the streets are quiet, but it's a Telluride that's timeless. And it seems to be an undiscovered town at that. A walk along any of its streets is a walk in another century. Even on the main street, grass sprouts from the curbs, and a dog slept on the sidewalk under a Welcome to Colorado sign.There didn't seem to be any tourist business. There is the town is, sort of pristine in its crumbling beauty and lost, far lost, in the past. . . .
> So are the lobby and the bar of the Sheridan Hotel. They're virtual time capsules; even the air in the lobby seems sealed in. Old hotel registers and records are strewn about on a table for inspection. There are rock specimens, leather chairs, brass spittons, and doors with stained glass. The lobby and bar are connected by a number of curious and vaguely sinister rooms. This, like all of Telluride, is for the purist time traveler.

Implicit in the observation were two salient points. Telluride was a gem of a place to visit, but Mrs. Lein's comments of 1953 were still valid: Not much had been done to encourage more people to come. That vital second lifeline still didn't exist.

By the early '60s an interest in jeeping through the spectacular San Juans led to the improvement of jeep routes through the mountains, and this brought a new kind of enthusiast to the area. The Black Bear Pass Road, still a demanding test of man and vehicle, was opened only to jeep traffic in 1959. Interest in the sport led to the formation of a local jeep club in 1963. Suddenly visitors had the opportunity to explore the rugged back country and see places some of the old-timers had never reached. To memories of dusty hotel registers, leather chairs, and musty rooms were added immense vistas of 14,000-foot peaks and sparkling valleys, antiquated cabins and deserted mines, and glimpses of dusty trails that hadn't been taken in fifty years.

In 1965 the slightly less difficult trail over Imogene Pass was opened to jeep travel — a beautiful route that climbed up to Bridal Veil Falls and Ingram Falls, then beyond to the ruins of the Smuggler and the Tomboy, past old Fort Peabody on Imogene pass and on down to Ouray. The less bold could opt for the "easy" Ophir Pass Road, which was as spectacular in scenery without offering the hairpin turns that long before had cost Will Webb his burro.

Disaster returned briefly at the end of 1964 when Christ Church burned and again in 1969 when Cornet Creek flooded one more time, causing $50,000 in damages. Christ Church was founded by Congregationalists but joined with other interests to form a community church in 1915. It eventually became the United Presbyterian Church in 1958. In an earlier day it had marked the spot where many a British minister had come to save the souls of hard-working, hard-living Cornish miners. Except for the steeple bell, the old landmark was a total loss.

The trend, however, had definitely changed for the better. In 1964 Congress declared that Telluride, because of its significance to the history of the United

Map Courtesy of the Telluride Transfer

Map of Jeep roads in the Telluride area (following page)

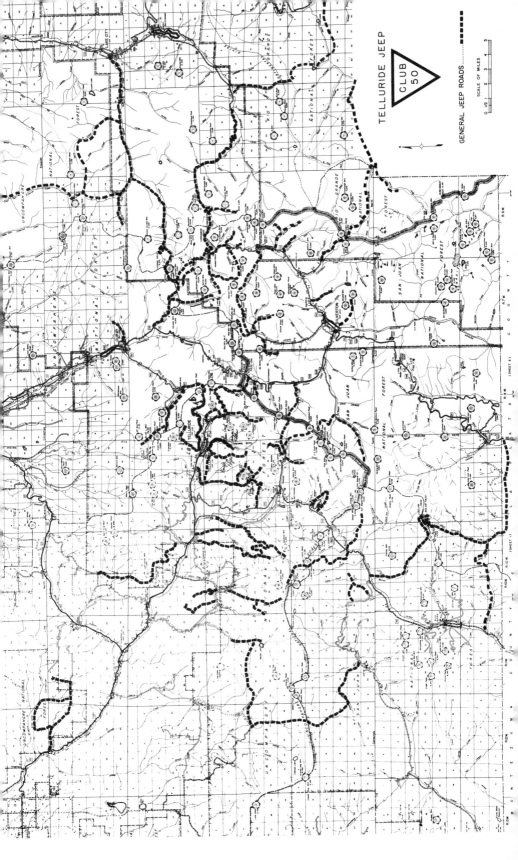

TELLURIDE JEEP

CLUB 50

GENERAL JEEP ROADS........

SCALE OF MILES
0 1/2 1 2 3 4 5

States, would become a National Historic Landmark, one of four places in Colorado to enjoy such distinction. The others are Cripple Creek, Silverton, and Central City. Telluride emerges from such distinguished company as the only town in continuous operation as a mining town since 1876, the year of Colorado's birth as a state.

The mid and late 1960s also brought new money and, curiously, the return of some mythical figures to the town. Hoping to attract $150,000 in deposits within eighteen months, the Bank of Telluride opened its doors in July 1969 for the first time since the days of Buck Waggoner. By the end of the first year of operation the bank had received more than $1 million, which suggested a lot of outside interest in the area, as Telluride's population was then barely over 600 residents.

Strangely enough, in a decade when men were walking in space and computers were making their way into everybody's business, reports of a return of the Tommyknockers began to increase. Tommyknockers belong to the world of elves and leprechauns, those "unreal" creatures whose existence you never experience unless you believe in them. They are underground creatures who first came to the area with the Cornish miners in the last century. How or exactly when they arrived, nobody knows, but some believe they stowed away in brass-bound trunks the men brought to Ophir.

Frank Richardson, who owned the Brooklyn Mine south of Red Mountain Pass was a strong believer in the little gremlins. "Hell, yes," he said late in 1964, "I was barring down one time, and I heard one of those little devils tapping on my bar. I stepped back, and the roof caved in." John German also experienced a Tommyknocker warning and heeded it barely in time. German and his partner were having lunch at the

Camp Bird Mine, unaware of an impending cave-in. German stepped back just as a rock fell. Before he could relay the warning, rocks struck and killed his friend.

Both Richardson and German could tell you why the Colorado National Guard failed to drop one shell out of twenty-six on their target on Mount Hayden in December 1964. The guardsmen had 155-millimeter howitzers, precision instruments, slide rules, caliphers, topographical maps, and an obervation plane. They had no way of knowing that the Tommyknockers in the San Juans were up there deflecting shells from the ridge because Mount Hayden is where the Tommyknockers cut down their Christmas trees.

It doesn't matter that the tale grows tall or that the more you listen the taller it is likely to grow. One must remember that this is the place where years ago the conductor leaned out the window as the train pulled into the depot and said with a grin, "This is it, folks, To Hell You Ride!" One must also keep in mind that, years before, two brothers who had fought in the Civil War stood in front of their place at San Miguel, met a troop of newcomers from somewhere in Wisconsin, and boldfacedly told them with a great gesture, "This is all ours!" One must also recall that this was a town that all too recently had been on the brink of death.

Amidst the mirth, the national recognition, and the inflow of new money, there was but one disquieting thought. What if the mines closed again? Not this year or next, maybe not even for the next decade, but if it happens some day, what then? Any rumor that the mines might be in trouble caused a shiver of panic. There had to be something else of substance in the area, but what?

More than one individual, casting an eye at the slope where L. L. Nunn had built his power line, pondered the possibility of a ski area. New words crept into the American vocabulary that drifted over the mountains in the 1960s into various minds in Telluride. Phrases like vertical drop, average annual snowfall, slope exposure, and deep powder were associated with a lot of coins dropping into the treasuries of Aspen, a new place called Vail, several other places in Colorado, as well as many resort towns back East and in California.

A handful of Telluride residents started talking about winter resort prospects. A few schemes were looked into. Once again it was a time for dreams — just as in 1875, when early prospectors followed rumors into the region, and when excited wealth-seekers built homes where the gas station outside town stands today and called the settlement San Miguel.

Then in 1969 a Californian came to town. He had been to Aspen frequently and had dreams as great as Fallon's and ideas almost as wild as those of Nunn and Otto Mears. He asked if he might have an evening to address the city council.

Courtesy of The Telluride Corporation

The mountains, always the reason for Telluride's isolation, provided the town's new lifeline, although few realized this in the '60s.

III. "SOMETHING BEAUTIFUL AND CONSTRUCTIVE"

Joe Zoline of Beverly Hills came to Telluride with a background in corporate law, manufacturing, and thoroughbred racing. He also had a strong record of financial success in his endeavors. He was one of many men with adventurous dreams, but he was one of a relative few with the means as well as the nerve to turn them into reality.

In 1955 Zoline bought a ranch in Aspen and started to raise cattle as a hobby. He watched Aspen develop over the years in a manner which wasn't entirely to his liking. It was at the moment when his discontent reached a new high that a friend suggested he have a look at Telluride, a place which was "like Aspen twenty-five years ago."

Zoline went to Telluride in 1968 and found a sleepy town at the end of a box canyon. It was pleasing beyond his expectations. In appearance the town had changed little since J. R. Humphreys' visit seven years before. A great wide street, no traffic lights, here and there an empty lot, simple Victorian houses, an occasional stray dog.

A big sheep ranch was for sale as a possible ski area site, and Zoline bought it. "I was feeling adventurous, and I wanted to do something beautiful and constructive," he said later. He bought the 900-acre ranch for $150,000 and realized he would need much more land to develop the great ski area he had in mind. By January 1969 he had increased his holdings to 3,500 acres of mountainside, with an option on another 1,000 acres.

Telluride when Joe Zoline arrived, a sleepy town at the end of a box canyon

It was in February that he spoke before the Chamber of Commerce, a group of about twenty people who represented the town's sixteen businesses. He told them what he hoped to do. Telluride's area would be "bigger than Vail, as large as Ajax, Aspen Highlands, and Buttermilk combined, and twice as big as Mammoth in California." The people looked at each other, they stroked their chins, and they looked at the floor. There was little response. In one form or another they had heard this kind of talk before. Nothing had ever come of it. Nothing was new.

It was a little like L. L. Nunn talking to his unbelieving public about alternating current, with the exception that people at least knew what skiing was. Zoline wasn't one to be put off by a less-than-enthusiastic reaction anymore than Nunn was. Nor was he one to repeat the steps of poor White, John Fallon's partner who lost his claim to the Smuggler for lack of a little assessment work. Zoline poured another $500,000 of hard work and good faith into the project and by the fall of 1972 had nearly $5 million tied up in Telluride.

The business community soon became excited by his project. New money, new ideas, and new people would be brought into town. Mrs. Mary Ellen Inama, a long-time resident who had served as San Miguel County judge and Telluride municipal judge, expressed the sentiments of a lot of people when she said, "I've seen the mines close and the people move away, and I know Telluride needs a shot in the arm. If the ski area or anything else would revive Telluride, I'm for it. We must grow, But we must control the growth."

Others weren't so sure. Look what had happened to Aspen — street people, drugs, trouble. We don't want that to happen here. In the fall of 1970 the people moved cautiously to allow Zoline to go ahead with his ideas. By a vote of 181 to 30 they gave him an option to purchase the town dump on the San Miguel River as a ski terminal site. If he didn't build by 1977, the town could buy it back at the same price of $1,000 per acre for the 3.6 acres. But Zoline had the green light. Another significant step was taken when the U.S. Forest Service made a long study of his preliminary plans and approved his location and scheme as an "official winter sports site."

Joe Zoline spared no effort, either physical or financial, in trying to guarantee that his "Big T" would be an admired achievement. His own aversion to the sprawl in Aspen was a strong factor in his plans to develop a place whose quality would enhance the attractiveness of the region. For a designer he hired Emile

Allais, the former French world champion skier who had subsequently designed eight of the world's premier resorts. Time was not of the essence; the accent was placed on doing the job well. The design that emerged had a planned completion date of 1990. At the base of the mountain would be a village for 8,000 people. In the meadows above would be small, year-round "ski-ranches" from which owners would be able to ski to the lifts and enjoy 60 miles of trails served by seventeen lifts for an eventual 17,000 skiers a day.

In the latter part of 1972 the first of the lifts opened. Automobiles began heading along Highway 145 and then south toward Ophir almost in the tracks of Butch Cassidy's escape in 1889. A short distance down the road and high above, skiers began to float down through some of the finest of Colorado's high, dry, fluffy powder and to drift along manicured packed trails. Not so very far from where early prospectors holed up for their first winter, people waxed skis, applied a layer of suntan lotion, and washed down a bite of cheese with a swallow of wine. Old names like Pick and Gad, Tomboy, Smuggler, Pandora, and Ophir Loop took on a new significance as the names of ski runs. To these were added more modern ones like First Love, for Colorado's long-time governor, and Allais Alley, for the man who had drawn it all with his pen.

On some parts of the mountain people preferred to simply admire the view before tackling the next part of the slope. The mind is free to drift 127 miles to the La Sal Mountains in Utah on a clear day, and then to turn north and absorb the saw-toothed needles of Mount Sneffels. On the east are the peaks blocking the mountains between Silverton and Ouray, which the men of the 1870s and 1880s crossed to settle Telluride. To the west the view is even more spectacular as the 14,250-foot summit of Mount Wilson lifts its lofty head above the rest of the San Juans. For those who prefer

Drifting down Ajax Glade

the solitude of cross-country skiing, the area offers stunning tours in terrain as beautiful as one could hope to find.

The fact that most of the surrounding land is national forest primitive area does much to quiet fears that the area might eventually spread out awkwardly and diminish the natural beauty of the region. The environs of Telluride enjoy a similar protected status, for the Uncompahgre National Forest Scenic Region surrounds most of the land which is not protected by sheer mountain walls. Telluride's designation as a National Historic Landmark carries with it federal sanctions which guarantee the continuation of the essential character of the town. To these the townspeople added

Courtesy of The Telluride Corporation

On a clear day . . . 127 miles to the La Sal mountains in Utah

Ski touring trails below Mount Wilson

further protection by adopting *in toto* the National
Building Code of 1970. This places a limit on the
height of commerical and residential buildings, pro-
hibits flashing or moving signs, and requires off-street
parking for new buildings.

The influx of money and the new interest in Telluride brought several significant changes to the town,
the greatest of which was a skyrocketing increase in
land prices. By 1972 speculation was as wild as in the
days when the mines were being discovered. Gold
fever had hit again, but without the physical hardship
of the original boom time. Other kinds of hardship did
arise, nevertheless. In 1969 the average assessed value
of an acre of irrigated land in San Miguel County was

$34.58. Two years later farmland near Telluride was selling for up to $10,000 an acre. Over a period of just one year, the cost of a lot in town rose from $100 to $1,000. Don O'Rourke, San Miguel County treasurer and a Telluride resident since 1905, found his house evaluation of $300 in 1971 had risen to $1,800 in 1972. By 1975 the value would increase again by a multiple of four. Many of the old Victorian houses that could have been bought for a few thousand dollars or less five years earlier had risen in price to $20,000. By 1973 even a small lot that would have sold for $10 in the '60s cost $9,000, and the little Victorian houses were at a minimum of $30,000. For anyone on a fixed income, sharp rises in taxes made it hard to stay in Telluride, and one by one the long-time residents began to leave. They received highly attractive sums of money for their property, and there was a certain attraction about spending the winter at a lower altitude, but to leave one's lifelong home was not an easy decision to make.

A more evident change was in the appearance of the town. Young people with money to invest came into Telluride willing to take a chance on starting new businesses. The main street soon featured new shops, boutiques, liquor stores, restaurants, craft centers, and a photography studio. The design was "rejuvenated Victorian," but with an eye to the preservation of the past. The new blended architecturally with the old, and each year the edges of philosophical differences lost some of their sharpness. In the latter part of 1974, Mrs. Homer Reid, curator of the county museum, said, "Well, I may leave one of these days, and I may not, but I'm sure not going to go until I'm good and ready. Besides, you know? There are some wonderful folks around here among these new people." Then she added quickly, "There are some real stinkers too, but that's true of any age people anywhere!"

Much has changed in Telluride, but there is much

. . . and on the way to Lizard Head

to indicate that the town remains essentially the same. In the early '70s the town marshall was a controversial figure in the best tradition of Jim Clerk. Marshall Everett M. Morrow, in 1972, would occasionally leave his patrol car home and make the rounds on a black horse. Morrow frowned on long hair. He dressed in cowboy boots and clothes, wore a Stetson, and carried his gun in a low-slung holster. His strict adherence to the letter of the law wasn't always appreciated by a younger, easy-going populace, but he met a less violent fate than many of his predecessors. He simply didn't get re-elected.

Also in 1972 Elvira Wunderlich became town clerk and, while browsing through record books, came across

an old revenue-raising ordinance that was apparently
still in effect. Ordinance No. 5 had been directed at the
licensing of entertainments, saloons, dance halls, parlors, and upstairs rooms of the red-light district. Except
for the repeal of the sections regarding madams in 1944
(since none were left) the ordinance had lain quietly on
the books over the years. In 1948 the language concerning licensing of any "shows, operas, lectures, ex-
hibitions, or performances of any kind" had been ex-
plicitly restored to the books.

The new clerk wasted no time in surprising the
Sheridan Opera House, which was performing melo-
drama during the summer, and the Nugget, Telluride's
only movie theater, with bills of $30 each. During the

Courtesy of The Telluride Corporation

A Fourth of July special slalom race at the Tomboy

Helicopter skiing in June — a far cry from what the old-timers knew

ensuing town council meeting the matter was brought up, and the town attorney said the old "red-light tax" was still in effect. Mrs. Betty Ruth Duncan, owner of the Nugget and also a councilwoman, moved to have what was left of the ordinance repealed. The vote was deadlocked, and it was left to Mayor Raymond Fancher to decide the issue. But what mayor could in good conscience vote agaist a red-light tax? The ordinance remained in effect.

The traditional celebration of the Fourth of July is still a big event in Telluride. If a slalom at the Tomboy has replaced the old drilling contests and fire-hose races, much of the same festive atmosphere is still there. The autumn Coloride spectacle, originally organized by the jeep club to attract tourists and show them the San Juans' annual display of fall colors, is still very much a part of the yearly agenda. The first Telluride Film Festival was held in 1974, an event that earned coverage from New York to Los Angeles. The festival featured an old nitrate film on the life of Tolstoy which had been tucked away in the attic of the Pekkarine Building and untouched for half a century. Also at the center of festivities was Gloria Swanson, who narrated one of her old films. Naturally there had to be an element of controversy, which flared up because of the presence of Leni Riefenstahl, who had long been called Hitler's mistress in Nazi Germany, although at her denial.

Even a kite flyer who jumped off one of the vertical cliffs and soared down to the lumberyard with ease provided but a momentary diversion from Hitler's supposed former companion. It is not surprising that the old-time residents weren't greatly attracted by the flying stunt, except for the successful landing. Old records recalled the same thing being attempted by some daredevil who tried to pre-empt the Wright Brothers in 1899. He too, jumped from the cliffs with wings attached to his arms, only to crash disastrously. Even without such stunts, the festival was called by the *New York Times* "the smallest, the most original, and in many ways the most stimulating of the major film festivals in the United States."

Most unchanged of all, however, is the striking character of the area itself. The tall cliffs and towering mountains that rise spectacularly above the small town meet the eye as magnificently and purely as they did in the early days. The zig-zag trail at the end of the canyon cuts the same pattern that was begun before Will Webb arrived, and the rivulets that give way to the creeks and rivers glow as clearly as ever. The sound of a pick has been replaced by the occasional hum of a power saw, and the clip-clop of horses and oxen has given way to the droning of engines and four-wheel-drive vehicles. Still, from behind the new paint or from a corner of a deserted lot peers an old facade or an antiquated empty brick building to testify that the character of the old Telluride is still there, changing but unchanged — still a time capsule, and one of the last living examples of the aura and savor of life as it was in our American West.

IV. A WALKING TOUR OF TELLURIDE

Umstead

Church

San Juan

Masons

Old Bel-mont

Jail

Good Time

Spruce St.

Roma

Lot

Bank of T.

Ladle

Toggery

Post Office

Shops

Sofio

Anderson Livery

Senate

Silver Bell

Cribs

Gold Belt

White House

Cozy Cor-ner

Idle Hour

Pick & Gad

Lost $

Pine St.

to Bear Creek Canyon

Miner's Hosp.

Fire St.

Town Hall

Museum

Painter

Galena St.

Columbia St.

Flora Olymp.

Title Realt.

Shop

Art

SMV Bank

Drugs

("Main Street")

Watson House Hotel

(former) Silver-jack

Fir St.

Big Swede

Monte Carlo

O'Rourke

Col'bine

Byers

BPOE

Cafe

Pekka-rine

Powder House

Shops

Dahl

Colorado Ave.

Oak St. Inn and Tavern

Movie

Lot

Sheridan

Pacific Avenue

Old Stone

Red-mond's

La Aloma

Oak St.

Court

Goose

Edge

(Start)

Park

S.M. Power

Davis

Aspen St.

Nunn In/H

Old School

Church

N

— — — Former Structure

We may go to London, Paris, Rome, Cairo, and other great centers of civilization where history was made and the course of man altered. There we may ponder the tradition behind Buckingham Palace, the place where the Bastille fell, the minds that ruled the Forum, and the secrets of the pyramids. To the right and left traffic buzzes, a new apartment complex goes up, or shabby ruins greet our eyes. The moment is lost. Abruptly the modern intrudes on our thoughts of the past.

So it is even in our country. Only with great perseverance can we follow the footsteps of the founders through the original small cities of Boston and Philadelphia. The site of the tree where the Sons of Liberty met has become an intersection; Samuel Adam's favorite tavern, a butcher shop.

Perhaps the less obvious but more important beauty of Telluride is that the setting has remained as it was in the days when its history was being lived. The street corners, buildings, and landmarks where so much happened in such a relatively short time would be easily recognized by the men and women who caused their existence and significance. With the exception of the main street, not a road has been paved in the town. There is not one traffic light. Only a few stop signs have changed the roads since the days of the horse and buggy.

Few people come to Telluride without wandering around its streets and wondering what happened here or there. We would like to add to the enjoyment of such moments by sketching a walk through the town. In doing so we will at first confine ourselves to the limits of the town boundary set in 1878, which still encompasses the heart of Telluride today. For those wishing longer walks, a few additional notes will be provided.

You will meet many people already discussed, along with a few other interesting characters who were less a part of the mainstream of the town's past. It will be necessary to stop at one of the old bawdy houses and at several of the great old bars — for historical purposes, of course.

To begin at the most conspicuous note of respectability, lets start at the *courthouse*. Still in active daily use, its easily noticed date of 1887 testifies this is one of the older buildings in town, dating from the year Columbia changed its name to Telluride. Next to the courthouse is the *Galloping Goose* No. 5, the weird result of Jack Odenpaugh's attempt to save the Southern in the early 1930s. *Infinite Edge*, separated from the Goose by an empty lot, was the scene of a murder back in the high-grading days. A man named Baisch, who then owned the drugstore, was murdered for his diamond ring when an angry miner claimed Baisch had swindled him by not paying enough for the miner's high-grade ore. The miner shot him in front of the building, took the ring and ran.

Across the main street, the *San Miguel Power Ass'n Inc.* operates from a brick building that was constructed by Congressman H. M. Hogg, who had his law offices there in 1899. According to one well-known Telluride story, Hogg, who pronounced his name "Hoag" rather than "hog," was married to a woman who was concerned about things such as name and position in life. The occasional mispronunciation of her name served to upset her to the point where one night, angry that her husband had been out late playing cards with the boys, she met him at the door and began to harangue him about his habits and the fact that their name was an embarrassment. Undaunted, he replied, "Listen, I'm a Hogg by birth and by nature, and I can't help it either. But you're a Hogg by choice!"

Next to the power company building is a small park, where a plaque commemorates and points toward where L. L. Nunn's power line ran. It also indicates Telluride's designation as a National Historic Monument. The date given on the plaque, 1963, indicates the year the work was initiated. Actual designation was in 1964.

We cross Oak Street and arrive at the *Sheridan Hotel*, long a Telluride landmark as prominent as the courthouse. The Sheridan was originally owned by the Sheridan mines, which owned a building that stood on the corner in the empty space next to the existing Sheridan. Originally a two-story building, the Sheridan added a third story in 1899, when it was in its second year of boasting about being lighted by electricity. As you stand in front of the Sheridan today you find yourself below the bleachers where William Jennings Bryan spoke in 1903. Inside, the old hotel retains some of its turn-of-the-century decor and atmosphere. The vast vestiges of the 1914 flood have finally disappeared. Ladies are no longer required to enter through a side door and await "the gentlemen's pleasure to dine."

Long ago the block starting with the Sheridan used to continue with a place called Scamps, then the Western Union building, and Spencer's Candy store, where the ladies went when the men went to the bars. All this has been replaced now, but the block culminates in a great, red sandstone building as it did then. This building, on the corner of Fir and Main, is now the *BPOE Lodge*, but if you look up toward the top of the structure you will see that originally it was the First National Bank of Telluride. The sandstone came from a quarry up on Cornet Creek during a period when the creek managed to stay within its creekbed for a few years.

The local chapter of the BPOE is still active, and a distinguished bar inside is still put to good use. The old eighteen-foot walnut bar was originally in the Cosmopolitan, but the bar and rail were moved to the Elks Club in 1938 by Silvio Oberto. Its fine old wood witnessed the announcement of many a gold strike in its heyday, as well as the sorry tale of many a less fortunate man.

In back of the BPOE Lodge there used to be an American Railway Express Station, where one night Bob Livermore, son of Colonel Livermore and brother-in-law of Bulkeley Wells, was sent to mail a horse. He had originally gone to the post office to mail the horse to Placerville. The officials refused and sent him to the express office. The clerk there couldn't believe the request, but he did comply with it.

Up from the BPOE Lodge on Fir street used to be the Columbine Hotel, which later became the Sheridan Annex. These no longer exist, but the site of *Joe Byers Photography Studio* can be detected by the engraving of his name in the sidewalk next to the BPOE Lodge on the Fir Street side.

Across the street on the block running from the Sheridan to the BPOE Lodge, we find the *Sunshine Pharmacy.* Just down Oak Street from the pharmacy is the charming *Dahl House,* a Victorian rooming house still in operation. The peculiar structure down from the Dahl House, with the two pointed roofs, belonged to the parents of George Rock, once a prominent Colorado Democrat. Rock at one time owned the Sheridan and did much to clean it up and preserve it when it was being neglected. He himself came to a drastic end, victim of a murderer on Skid Row in Denver.

To return to the main street, we find next to the

pharmacy a series of shops, and then a fairly large brick
building. This is the *Pekkarine Building*, where an old
nitrate film on Tolstoy was found in 1974. At various
times the building housed many stores and shops. The
Pekkarines lived upstairs, accumulating period pieces
of the early twentieth century that were given to the
museum during the settling of the estate in 1974. In
this block some fifty years ago was the *San Miguel Examiner* and on its left as you faced it, the old
Metropolitan Theater. The brick building on the right
(on page 33) in the old photograph is no longer in existence.

Almost, but not quite, on the corner is a long brick
building which now contains the *Excelsior Cafe*. If you
walk around the side of the building you may be able
to make out part of the word "Hardware," a remnant
from the days when the building was occupied by
Thomkins & Christie, a hardware supplier that operated in Telluride, Cripple Creek, and other mining
camps in Colorado.

Before crossing Fir Street to look at the next block
on Colorado, look down to Fir to the intersection and
the remains of an old stone building. Here, just beyond
the present station site, was *Redmonds*. If you had
been there on March 10, 1911, or on many other cold,
blustery March nights, you could have looked in on the
annual *Mule Skinner's Ball*. One afternoon a few years
earlier you could have observed a train car of unionists
being marched into Redmond's by the Citizens Com-
mittee and the National Guard.

In the same block, near *La Aloma*, Fir Street
crossed the railroad tracks. It was here than Lee Long
lost his life in 1920.

From the intersection at Fir and Colorado one can
also look up Fir to find the *Telluride Art Gallery*,
which originally was the telephone company building.
This used to be the Wagner's Art Studio, founded by a

family that moved to Telluride from New Hampshire in 1964. Although the Wagners no longer live in Telluride, their original paintings, which capture much of the spirit of Telluride and the San Juans, are still available here, along with various books on Colorado and the West.

When we cross Fir and enter the next block we find a large wooden building, once the *Silverjack Restaurant*, occupying the south side of the street; otherwise, little else is there. At one time the southeast corner of Fir and the main street was the site of the first courthouse, which was replaced by the present courthouse in 1887. At the far corner of the block was once the Watson House Hotel, but this too is gone. Of some interest to the present, however, is the bed of the *printing press*, to the left of the Silverjack as you face it, which printed the first edition of the newspaper in 1881 after the snow was brushed away.

Across the street, on the north side of the main street, we have several points of interest. The *drugstore* on the corner, for example, was once the home of the *Telluride Club*, a small group of men who met above the drugstore and played cards. On the wall of the clubroom was a painting of a nude, supposedly painted by a young artist during gold-fever days. According to the tale, the artist had lily-white hands that were without callouses. His demeanor was too artisitc to inspire anyone to grubstake him, and the young man soon ran out of money. One of the girls who worked the line on Pacific Avenue agreed to help him by posing for the painting, which he then sold. Subsequently he found a good claim, he married the girl, and they bought a home on the north side of town and settled into a life of respectability.

After many travels around town, the painting came to rest in the Telluride Club. No one claimed it when the club closed in 1948, so Frank Wilson, figuring it was abandoned, put it in his drugstore. One day an old miner walked in and said, "Audrey!" The miner said he had owned the painting long ago and had never given it up. A quarrel broke out, which Wilson ended by grabbing his gun and chasing the miner out of the store. Claims were never settled to everyone's satisfaction — including the BPOE, who felt the painting belonged to the whole town. Audrey, however, remains in the Wilson family, although not in the drugstore.

The old-fashioned soda fountain is still in the drugstore, now the office of the Telluride Ski Area, along with "Dad" Painter's old safe.

There was at one time a bowling alley in the building occupied by the drugstore. Of greater interest is the building next door, which was the *San Miguel Valley Bank*, the site of Butch Cassidy's first robbery in 1889. The somewhat more likely looking bank building with the Greek columns just down the street was also a bank, but this was the old *Bank of Telluride*, the intended beneficiary of Buck Waggoner's 1929 scheme.

It was on this street that Umstead was shot in the back when the *Tremont Bar* was there, and as you pass the title and realty companies before arriving at the old Bank of Telluride, you would have once seen *Harry Miller's barbershop*. Harry Miller's wife's family arrived in Telluride in 1881, when it was still Columbia, and she was active in the hospital work of the early days. One room in the museum is devoted to bedroom artifacts which she donated from the house she and her husband once occupied on the northeast corner of Spruce and Columbia. To a certain extent her personal life had its share of tragedy. Her two brothers both died violently; one was the Umstead shot in the Tremont, the other was one of the men killed in the Liberty Bell avalanche of 1902. A pre-1910 photograph of Miller's barbershop shows how much the block changed over the years; the Belmont saloon (one of several by the name), the boot shop, and the barbershop have long since disappeared.

The volumes inside the title company contain every mining claim ever filed in Columbia or Telluride. Over the years, clerks in the office have found themselves trying to sort out former claims concerning an ambiguous "rock outcrop" or a "gnarled old pine" that no longer exists "50 paces away." "Dad" Painter's old desk and his huge safe from Ohio with the romanticized scenery on the front used to be title company fixtures, but the desk was sold and the safe is now in the office of the Telluride Ski Area.

We come to the end of this block by approaching the *Flora Dora Building* and *Olympic Sports*. Here, in the '90s, was the *"Up-to-Date Outfitter," W. B. Van Atta*. This was a necessary stop for the miner needing to spruce up for his Saturday night fling. On a big evening a place like Van Atta's might sell $2,000 worth of merchandise.

Rather than continue down the main street let's wander to Pacific Avenue to see what remains of the spiciest section in old Telluride — "the line." As we walk down Pine we can immediately see a large building beyond Pacific Avenue on the left-hand side. This was the well-known *Pick and Gad*. (A gad was a Cornish term for a pointed iron bar used by miners to loosen ore.) On the corner between the Pick and Gad and Pacific Avenue was the *Idle Hour*. Opposite these two popular places were the *Big Swede* and the *Monte Carlo*. Of these, only the Pick and Gad remains. The dirt road that continues past these buildings leads to seven waterfalls and Bear Creek Canyon, a beautiful area that provided some of the background scenery for the filming of *The Unsinkable Molly Brown*. This and *How The West Was Won* were two of the popular films made in the Telluride area.

Turning left on Pacific Avenue we see three of the

cribs that were in use during wilder days. It was in a building like this that Jess Munn found Marshall Gigline with his girl and subsequently shot him. It was also in such a building that Jim Clark died after his unknown murderer shot him. Across from the cribs were the *Cozy Corner, White House,* and *Gold Belt.*

The line ran some distance down Pacific Avenue. If, upon arriving at Spruce Street, we turn left and head back toward the main street we come first to the *Silver Bell* and then the *Senate.* The original building was constructed in the 1880s and at first consisted of a two-story place called *McPherson's Rooming House,* which adjoined the Silver Bell saloon. On July 4, 1890, a disgruntled customer set fire to the Silver Bell, and the rooming house was severely damaged. Using material salvaged from the original structure, Barney Gabardi and a partner rebuilt the structure and ran it as a saloon and gambling hall. The original brass rail was found in the basement, and this was put in place. The Senate was bought in 1965 by Mr. and Mrs. William Hammer, who planned to remodel it as a home and art galley, but they sold it to Terry and Steve Catsman, who opened it in 1973. The Senate operated during prohibition but was closed from 1935 until 1973.

The Senate today provides a superb example of what can be done to preserve and recreate the flavor of the past. Operating as a bar and restaurant, the Senate is appropriately Victorian in decor, with the original roulette wheel, poker table, and faro table, salvaged from the fire. The bar dates from 1880 and still has the brass rail and spittoons. A bullet hole in the floor remains from a long-ago evening when a sheriff lost an ear in a gunfight. The basket suspended near the entrance served many a "basket case" in the mines.

Across the street from the Senate is the jail, next to the *Good Time Society,* which some recalled as being the *Dizzy Crib.* Next to the jail and back a bit is the old

Belmont. The Belmont used to be at the edge of the street, like the jail, but the property belonged to the Masonic Temple, and the lodge wanted the building torn down. George Kovich, the owner who was then 70, sawed the building in half and moved the structure back onto his own land, and there it stands now.

We approach the main street once again. On the right at the corner is the *Masonic Temple.* On the roof of the *San Juan Cafe* next door hid the gunman who felled Jim Clark. We won't proceed any farther east along the main street, for there is little else to see of the town, but two blocks down was the site of the *Stubbs and Jakeway Opera House.* Travelling stock companies performed there, and it was also used for dances. Downstairs in the same building was the *F. D. Work* interest, which was composed of a few shops. An old photo of the F. D. Work place shows the railroad cutting across the street here, from which point it continued to Pandora.

If we stand at the intersection of Spruce and the main street and look back toward the Sheridan, it is easy to imagine the daily commotion caused by freighters like Dave Wood when they lined their donkeys the length of the town to load the animals for the mines. The wide spacious main street through town still holds an attraction. It is easy to sympathize with those prospectors who left San Miguel for Columbia, "where a team of six oxen could turn easily in the streets."

Before turning up the main street toward the Sheridan, note the gargoyle on the brick building just off the corner. If there is any significance in the gargoyle other than decoration, it is unknown today. The building once housed the *Brunswick Saloon,* which was of greater significance to a thirsty miner than some imaginary creature on the roof.

Across the street is the *Roma,* and inside is one of

the finest period pieces in Telluride, a beautiful bar and backbar built in the 1860s by Brunswick-Balke-Collender Company. The bar is made of carved walnut and is twenty feet in length. The French mirrors of the backbar give the entire ensemble a height of twelve feet, but it is the quality rather than the size which is impressive. Some years ago, when an offer was made to buy the entire bar and backbar, each of the exquisite French mirrors was valued at over $1,500. The offer wasn't accepted, and there has been no talk of sale since. The bar has one blemish which was caused by a coin. This has always been attributed to "Old Joe King." King walked into the Roma, took his last silver dollar, and threw it on the bar. He ordered drinks for all as far as his money could go, which, at two beers for a quarter, wasn't too bad. The customers drank to Joe's better luck in the future, and, thanks to obtaining a lease on the Camp Bird Mine at Ouray, he eventually became a prosperous man.

Next to the Roma was the old *O. K. Clothing* place, and next to that was another of the popular places, the *Cosmopolitan*. As we approach the new *Bank of Telluride,* look for a moment across the street again. In the large building now housing the *Lost Dollar Saloon* and *Sofio's* was one of the greatest bootleg whiskey centers in town. In fact, at one time there were three bars in that building; it must have been one of the wettest buildings in Colorado. There was also a livery stable and a post office. The bars paid the post office to locate there. The bootleg operation was the one where the soda jerk kept the revenue man busy while his cohorts made appearances presentable downstairs. By the time the investigator reached the basement to watch the friendly card game over ice-cream sodas, the white lighting had been shoved into the post office next door. One of these bars, *The Diamond,* was the scene of a lot of gambling and had a big bar that was liked by the more serious drinkers.

At the corner of the building, above Jeremiah's, was the *National*. This was the former home of the Roma bar and in its day was as popular an eating place as the Cosmopolitan or Sheridan.

Continuing past the new bank we find the *Toggery*. At one time this was the Knights of Pythias Hall. The Odd Fellows met there, as did woodcraft groups. The block is completed with the *post office*, which occupies the site of the first post office the town had. Here, one day in 1887, came a letter that requested Columbia to help clarify postal difficulties by changing to another name.

If we turn up Pine Street toward Columbia we can see a brick building on the left-hand side of the intersection that served as the *Miner's Union Hospital* from 1902–04, built in 1902 by the Western Federation of Miners. Subsequently it was used as the post office and for a time as the BPOE Lodge. Today it has become the home of a washeteria and a community owned radio station.

After passing an empty lot we arrive at the *Fire Station* and *Town Hall*. The building now serving as Town Hall is the original schoolhouse constructed in 1883. Behind it was the fire station. Thinking back to the fire truck disaster of 1920, it is easy to reconstruct an image of horses bolting out of the station, gathering speed all the way down Fir, and finally crashing onto the train track where it crossed below Pacific Avenue.

It is fair to say that a visitor with time for only one historic point of interest should go to our next stop, the *museum*. Officially it is known as the San Miguel County Museum, but is contents relate more to Telluride and its area than to the county as a whole. The curator is Mrs. Arlene Reid, and she seems to have some connection with every item on display. There are pictures, old lanterns from narrow-gauge days, gaming tables, slot machines, an old safe, an iron mine bicycle, a 1932 hair dryer and permanent wave machine, mine tools, an enormous old map of claims, silverware, glasses, a restored kitchen, a bedroom with period pieces, a library, clothes, a schoolroom, operating table, dentist chair, wheelchair, saddles, horseshoes, sewing implements, musical instruments, and reminders of World War I.

It is interesting to go to the museum and simply wait for some visitor whose uncle was a bartender in the old days or whose grandfather worked as a roust-about at the Pandora. Stories will be swapped and pertinent old photos pointed out. Perhaps at the end there will be one more face identified at last in one of the old pictures.

Some of the old stories that emerge are fascinating, some raise an eyebrow, but all reflect what is and was Telluride. One of the old legends that can be pointed out from the museum's hillside vantage point, especially in autumn, is the story of the *coonskin*, a patch of aspen trees located on the opposite slope on Boomerang Hill.

The story dates from the early days of the Ute Indians when a party under Chief Te-oe op San went up the canyon on an exploratory mission. It was September, and the Indians were attracted by the bright yellows, golds, and oranges of the turning aspen. One of the braves spotted a raccoon, which he shot. The animal ran, trying to escape the pain and survive the wound. As he ran blindly by, the aspens called out to their friend, asking what had happened. The raccoon ran on and eventually died at the spot where he had been shot. The Indian brave skinned his kill, and the Indians left.

The aspens went into mourning for their friend. Out of respect for his memory they refused, however, to don dark, somber colors, which would make everything sad, but chose joyous colors of yellow, gold, and orange. The next day the Indians were terrified by the vision of a raccoon outlined in the trees. The head pointed to the northwest, the skin was outstretched, and the tail pointed toward the southeast. The frightened Indians fled, and the Ute brave killed himself in grief.

Each year when yellow leaves appear on the quaking aspen, the trees along the route taken by the wounded raccoon don their summer hues for the blood the little animal shed on their roots. The result is that the leaves of the aspen change color earlier than those on the rest of the hillside. The outline of the coonskin has thus become the traditional first sign of autumn for Telluride. A little myth, a bit of fantasy, and in the beauty of September perhaps some truth: such is Telluride, our extraordinary legacy where every-day living was a tall tale in itself.

The museum was built in 1893 as the Miners' Hospital. Mrs. Harriet Fish Backus, writer of *Tomboy Bride*, gave birth to the first baby in the hospital in 1909. The building served as a hospital until 1964, when it closed for two years. It opened as a museum in 1966.

If we now head back down Fir Street toward Columbia we will find on our right-hand side, opposite the present city hall, the lovely old *house where "Dad" Painter* lived. Across Columbia was the *home of Don O'Rourke*, county treasurer and a man who has shared many a tale of Telluride over the years. Don recalls his very early days selling newpapers along the line, and he remembers playing cards with Buck Waggoner the night before he disappeared. Don won $35 playing panguingue, and Buck paid him with a check which, of course, bounced. Don's home was once lived in by "One-Armed" Sampson, the man in charge of employment at the Tomboy. Sampson killed himself in the house. There is supposed to be a bullet lodged in the wall, but it has never been found.

Continue west along Columbia and you come to the *Oak Street Inn* and *Tavern.* These are on the site of the *Old Methodist Church,* built in 1900. The church became a recreation hall in 1915 and had a hardwood floor where basketball was played. If we turn the corner and head down Oak Street we can pass the movie house, built around 1914 and "not so old as people think," according to Don O'Rourke. We then arrive at the main street and return to our point of beginning.

If we continue west on Columbia we come to the *E. L. Davis house* on the northwest corner of Columbia and Oak. This was once the site of a hospital. It is sometimes called the Wagner house, after a woman who cleaned the attic and basement. She later moved to a hotel in Arizona to have valets and butlers. A man named Erickson once lived across the street and, like One-Armed Sampson committed suicide. Erickson jumped out of a bucket on the Liberty Bell Tram.

At Columbia and Aspen, on the northeast corner, is a house with a happier history. Here lived the fellow who struck it rich, married a girl from the line, and lived happily ever after. On the northwest corner is the house where *L. L. Nunn* lived, and next to that is what used to be his *Institute.* Approximately across from the institute, on the south side of Columbia, was the First Congregational Church, now *Christ Church,* and further down Columbia on the north side is the *old schoolhouse* built in 1895.

In back of the old school, up on Galena, is the house that was boarded in half by McMann when he got divorced. Even the piano was divided. McMann was an eccentric in a day when to stand out as such took a little doing. Born on Pacific Avenue, he was a true native, and he grew up to become known as a gay blade and good lawyer. Then he suddenly stopped washing and took to hauling coal. One time, when his wife was having a baby, their mare was having a foal. McMann stayed with the foal.

McMann was once the county commissioner. But when he went off the deep end he ate out of the same breakfast bowl day in and day out and looked like the coal he was hauling. If his clothes needed mending he would use white thread. If he had to buy a new truck he would put the old body on the new truck. Wherever the truck wound up at the end of the day he would crawl under it and sleep. One of his buildings down by the icehouse became his regular quarters. On one occasion he was known to leave $3,000 in a sack and wait two weeks before picking it up. A year might go by before he would cash a check, and if he hadn't had to pay taxes he might have waited longer.

There was another notable character who lived in this part of town. On the corner next to the old school is a *quonset building* which is now the Telluride Community Center. Opposite the quonset is a brown house which was once a mule barn. The barn was eventually owned by Martin Anderson, who was the recording secretary of the Miners' Union and manager-superintendant of the Liberty Bell and later the Tomboy. Anderson was highly respected by the community and by the miners. His prominence was such that on one occasion a Swedish miner taking out citizenship papers, when asked, "Who is the President?" replied, "Martin Anderson."

There are other points of interest, but not within short walking distance. Several blocks to the west, between North Taylor Street and North Watson Street, was Telluride's only brewery — or perhaps it is more accurate to say its only legitimate one. Bought by Mr. Wichmann in 1903, the Telluride Brewery lasted until prohibition days. It served the entire town, as well as

Rico and Silverton, which were reached by wagon over
Ophir Pass. Bottling, steaming, and labelling were all
done by hand by Mr. Wichmann and one or two assis-
tants who would work an eight-to-ten-hour day de-
pending on the demand.

Out of town on the east is the *cemetery*, the land for
which was donated long ago by George Andrus when
his baby died. As with other old cemeteries, there is
much of the local past etched into the weathered tomb-
stones, some of them exceedingly simple, others quite
ornate.

Before leaving Telluride, if indeed you must, complete your tour with a ride up to the Tomboy or the
Alta. It is here you will truly feel the isolation experienced by the early miners. One side is still rocks and
the other still offers eternity. Take a jeep or let the
local jeep company take you. For hikers and backpack-
ers the only limitation is one's imagination. Some
travellers may feel more comfortable doing the jeep
trails on foot, and many jeep trips end up that way.

Be sure to ask in town about high-county road conditions before you go, regardless of the time of year,
and remember that bad weather can move in fast in the
mountains. Remember, too, that here you must expect
the unexpected. In this world of splendid peaks and
distant views, of Tommyknockers and Galloping
Geese, of ancient legends and dusty streets, you are
surrounded by the ghosts of men and women who lived
and died by such a rule, and in doing so built Telluride
from pick to powder.

Postscript

And so it was that Telluride entered the mid 1970s. As the decade passed and the '80s came along, the ski area became completed, new lodges went up, and new homeowners came into town. Ironically, at a time when gold set record high prices internationally, the mines shut down again. Telluride, ever a home for the resourceful person, added more festivals to the agenda, which continue to bring visitors for weekends of wine, bluegrass, rock n' roll, jazz, chamber music, dance, hang gliding, and mountain films, in addition to its by now well established Film Festival.

Unfortunately, escalating prices and severe winters have continued to drive some of the old time residents to more moderate climes. Don O'Rourke has gone; so has Alta Cassieto. Miners have had to look elsewhere for work, thus severing another link with the town's past. Arlene Reid still keeps things in order at the museum, and others like Elvira Wunderlich are still at home in Telluride, but over the years the character of the town has continued to change as the rest of the world discovers Telluride.

Yet, while there may be new people and different facades, coats of paint and new construction, something essential remains unaffected. Walk down to the old station on a clear night when a cool breeze fills the air and you will find yourself all alone. The station is boarded up, as it has been for a long time, and plenty of signs will tell you to keep out. Here, for a moment, thoughts of old trains come readily to mind, great old steamers chugging their way in, bringing an earlier world to Telluride. In the great vastness of this still isolated canyon, the cliffs still soar and dominate, the trails still lead to places worth one's while to explore. Yes, the time capsule has opened; times have changed. But here in Telluride, still to a far greater extent than in most towns you'll ever find, you can feel some of the old West and a way of life that will not come our way again.